# Share Valuation Handbook:
## Techniques for the valuation of shares in private companies

Fourmat Publishing

# Share Valuation Handbook:
## Techniques for the valuation of shares in private companies

by Leslie Livens, ATII, AITI
of Moores and Rowland

London
**Fourmat Publishing**
1986

ISBN 0 906840 98 8


First published December 1986


**Reprinted January 1988**

© 1986 Leslie Livens
Published by Fourmat Publishing, 27 & 28 St Albans Place,
Islington Green, London N1 0NX
Printed in Great Britain by
Billing & Sons Limited, Worcester

# Foreword

I know of no financial technical subject that gives rise to such differences of opinion and argument as share valuation principles. Perhaps that is what makes the subject so fascinating. This book was started with the object of simplifying the subject-matter; I hope that at least it presents the broad techniques in a useful format, and will assist in the preparation of meaningful share valuation reports.

My gratitude goes to Victor Clements, David Garlick, Dr Victor Baker and David Trill, all of Moores and Rowland, Chartered Accountants, for their valuable assistance, but I must take responsibility for any shortcomings in the book. And if any readers simply have different opinions from those expressed in this book — well, an opinion is, after all, only an opinion is it not?

Leslie Livens
Cliffords Inn
London                                        November 1986

Of valuers . . .

> "It seems to me that their opinions are indeed properly described as guess-work, though of course it is intelligent guesswork . . ."

> Mr Justice Danckwerts, Re Holt, Holt v IRC

# Contents

# Table of cases

# Chapter 1

# Introduction

## 1.1 Background

Many occasions give rise to a valuation of shares in a private company and most, if not all, have some immediate or future tax consequence.

Whenever there is a direct tax consequence it will be necessary to prepare a formal valuation report (see Chapter 9) for submission to the Inland Revenue; and in transactions which are not at arm's length, that valuation may differ from the value that one or other of the parties to the transaction has in mind. Differences of this nature can and do arise, and so far as this book is concerned the sections dealing with fair value (2.10), oppression of minorities (2.14) and capital gains tax (8.2) may be of particular interest.

Arriving at a share valuation on paper is not always the end of the matter, certainly not in the case of valuation for tax purposes. A tax valuation has to be agreed by the appropriate Inspector of Taxes or other Inland Revenue officer (Chapter 10), and he may well (and probably will) refer the valuation to Shares Valuation Division of the Inland Revenue. This department is staffed by highly experienced examiners who have available to them a vast amount of information on share valuation matters, including files accumulated over many years dealing with settled valuations of private companies of all shapes and sizes, ages and complexity. They also have access to information concerning the company whose shares are being valued, including details of any previously notified dealings in the shares. Through years of specialisation they have acquired excellent negotiating skills.

Without careful and thorough preparation, it is most unwise to commence negotiation with Shares Valuation Division. Unfortunately, if a difference of opinion does arise between valuer and Shares Valuation Division the correspondence can run on for months. It is therefore important to collect complete and unambiguous evidence supporting any tax valuation; and the background to the valuation — ie the precise purpose of the valuation, the principles adopted and the calculation — should be presented clearly in the valuation report.

## 1.2 Valuer's opinions

A fully detailed formal valuation report is not always required — such as where, under a company's Articles of Association, the company's auditor (acting as expert, not arbitrator) is required to state his "opinion" as to the "fair value" of the company's shares. This matter is dealt with at 2.10. The point here is that some valuers find it less inhibiting simply to give an opinion statement (a "non-speaking" valuation) rather than a full valuation report (a "speaking" valuation). The reason is that the cases that require an "opinion" are often ones where the value is important to two separate parties with separate interests; whatever value is arrived at one party is likely to be dissatisfied and it is not inconceivable that litigation might ensue. The more detail that is presented, the more can be brought into dispute. This is not to say that the "non-speaking" valuation could not be set aside by the court, but provided that the valuer has taken proper care in determining his opinion at least he cannot become the personal target of an aggrieved party. Not, that is, unless it can be shown that the valuer had acted negligently or fraudulently, or a mistake, miscarriage or error of principle is evidenced.

Lord Denning's judgment in the case of *Campbell* v *Edwards* usefully summarises the position, simply stated, that a valuer when acting as expert can be liable for negligence, whereas if acting as arbitrator he cannot be so liable. In *Collier* v *Mason*, despite "perhaps an exorbitant valuation", the Master of the Rolls said "I cannot say it amounts to evidence of fraud, mistake or miscarriage".

In summary, the valuer himself is not personally liable unless he is dishonest or negligent; the valuation, however, can be impeached for fraud, mistake or miscarriage. Where an opinion is given, if the valuation is a "non-speaking" valuation the court can only interfere "if the figure itself is so extravagantly large or so inadequately small that the only conclusion is that he must have gone wrong somewhere"; if the valuation is a "speaking" valuation then "on matters of opinion, the courts will not interfere, but for mistake of jurisdiction or of principle, and for mistake of law, including interpretation of documents and for miscarriage of justice, the courts will interfere". Both quotations are from Denning LJ in *Dean* v *Prince*. A valuer can effectively turn a "non-speaking" valuation into a "speaking" valuation if he chooses to disclose the method of his valuation.

Finally, the "opinion" of the valuer is only relevant in this context where it is given under the terms of a contractual arrangement between parties.

Where a share valuation is prepared for tax purposes, the valuer's "opinion' is clearly not binding on the Inland Revenue until agreement is reached. If two unconnected parties ask for an independent assessment of market value for the purpose of a disposal by one party to the other it is likely that, on the grounds that the bargain is made on terms completely at arm's length, the valuation would have to be accepted by the Inland Revenue as the end of the matter (but see, for example, Capital Gains Tax Act 1979 ss.25 and 26 (value shifting)). If the parties are related or connected in tax terms, the Inland Revenue would still pursue its own valuation of the market value and the normal appeal procedures would be available in case of a dispute.

Some of the more common instances for valuing private company shares are discussed below.

## 1.3 Sale/Purchase

On a straightforward sale or purchase of company shares there is clearly a need to value what is being bought and sold. The number of shares being sold as a percentage of the entire issued share capital is relevant as will be seen at 3.7, but the other circumstances surrounding the transaction must be made clear to the valuer because, either for taxation or company law purposes, there could be wider consequences. Chapter 8 covers the various tax situations and in any share transaction the parties should satisfy themselves of the tax position before committing themselves.

Problems can arise where the transaction takes place for a consideration other than cash, or at an undervalue or overvalue (see Chapter 8). The transaction may be a compulsory purchase under the Companies Act 1985 s.461(2)(d), which will also require a valuation.

## 1.4 Variation of rights

If there is a variation in the rights attaching to any shares it is probable that value has been removed or added with a consequential increase or reduction elsewhere.

There may well be commercial reasons supporting a variation of rights and there may be actual consideration passing, but whatever the case it is wise to check the capital gains tax rules relating to value-shifting and depreciatory transactions. Capital transfer tax/ inheritance tax may also be in point if the value of someone's estate has been reduced. If the variation is in respect of shares held by employees Taxes Act 1970 s.183 and Finance Act 1972 s.79, in relation to share opportunities, may apply (see Chapter 8).

In all these events a valuation will be necessary — probably by reference to the reduction or increase in value. But, if the prospective variation had already been taken into account in an earlier transaction it may be that there is no further tax consequence and no further valuation requirement.

It is important to understand the purpose of any variation in rights, which may have been contingent upon the happening of another event (such as targeted profits being achieved), or simply the desire to make a gift of value.

## 1.5 Financing

A valuation may be necessary if shares are to be held by a bank or other financial institution as security for a loan. The creation of a mortgage or charge over the assets of the company may affect the value of the shares in issue notwithstanding that the creation of the charge will bring new finance into the company. This will depend upon all the circumstances, not least of which will be the reasons for raising the borrowings. Some financing arrangements call for a subscription of new equity and the issue of new shares and/or debentures. The valuation basis for a new issue may be quite different from that for existing shares. Thus a minority shareholding subject to pre-emption rights should not be valued for tax purposes in quite the same way as, for example, risk capital put up in tandem with a convertible secured loan by a financial institution that may be investing in a number of companies on the basis that a small proportion will be outstandingly successful. See also 1.8 below.

## 1.6 Flotation

Prior to a flotation of shares the "value" can vary daily because of a host of totally extraneous matters — mostly to do with the perceived mood of a special type of institutional investor. If any estate planning is undertaken, such as transferring shares into trust prior to a flotation (and such planning often is left to this late stage), there will be a separate valuation exercise under the traditional principles of tax valuation rules which, depending upon how close the events are to each other, may be influenced by the price at which the stock eventually floats. This matter is discussed in 2.12, and see 1.8 below.

## 1.7 Buy-back of shares

Under the Finance Act 1982 Sch.9, a company may in the right circumstances acquire its own shares from a "retiring" shareholder and effectively cancel the shares. The rules that allow this to happen with a relief from income tax are complex and strict and a valuation on normal principles will be necessary.

## 1.8 Demergers and management buy-outs

On any fundamental alteration to the capital structure of a company, be it simply a reorganisation of share capital or a more traumatic piece of financial surgery there will be a requirement from both the commercial and taxation points of view to value what is going, what is coming in, and what is staying. Not only can these matters be complicated, they can also have tax consequences ranging across the entire spectrum. Note especially the requirement to value non-cash consideration received by a public company (not necessarily a quoted company) for a share issue (Companies Act 1985 s.103). Typically, in a demerger situation new money is being attracted from a bank or other institutional investor. The value is therefore often determined more by reference to the practice of that particular investor than by any market value concept. That value would not reflect the true open market value on the date of the demerger, but more a basic value, after infusion of new money, by reference to which the future performance can be judged.

## 1.9 Share schemes

Whenever approved or unapproved share option and incentive schemes are introduced (including a transfer of shares from an existing shareholder to an employee as such), the shares must be valued for income tax and capital gains tax purposes (see Chapter 8). In the case of an approved scheme the Shares Valuation Division will probably agree a value specifically for the purposes of the scheme and for no other purpose — ie a "without prejudice" valuation agreed to save the time and trouble that would attend a full valuation. This value could be used only for the purposes of the share scheme for employees in determining any future income tax or capital gains tax liability arising out of the scheme.

## 1.10 Matrimonial proceedings

The value of shares held by either party to matrimonial proceedings may be relevant. A valuation may have implications for the future even if no immediate transfer of shares takes place, because a value for the shares at a point in time has been struck. Tax market value rules would apply in relation to any tax implication, but for determining the value of one party's assets for the purposes of divorce, the open market value, untainted by the specific tax value assumptions (as explained in 8.4), would be taken.

## 1.11 Death

Valuation of shares on the shareholder's death will be required to establish the value for probate purposes as well as for capital transfer tax or inheritance tax and capital gains tax. Although no capital gains tax is chargeable on death, valuation is necessary to establish the new base cost in the hands of the beneficiary; see Chapter 8.

## 1.12 Other occasions

Valuations may be necessary on a distribution by a trust and also for the purpose of various "deemed disposal" transactions for tax purposes (dealt with in Chapter 8).

## 1.13 The starting point

Assuming the principles (Chapter 2) are clear, the

starting point is the shares themselves (see Chapter 3). Having identified the rights and restrictions attaching to the shares, the next step is to decide whether the number of shares held will direct the valuer to one or other of the valuation bases (see 3.7). A minority interest will indicate the Dividend Basis (Chapter 4), a majority interest the Earnings Basis (Chapter 5); although it may be appropriate to adopt a Hybrid Basis (Chapter 7) where the valuer is not satisfied that one of the other bases is wholly appropriate. An Asset Basis (Chapter 6) will be appropriate in a case of impending liquidation or if there is extraordinary asset value involved.

The valuer needs a wide range of skills, including a knowledge of the legal principles of valuation. He must be able to interpret a balance sheet and understand trading and profit and loss accounts. In any particular case, he must understand the basis adopted for depreciation, bad debts and reserves, and the accounting practices adopted in general and in particular. He must be able to identify and distinguish extraordinary expenditure and exceptional expenditure, and he must be able to take a view, often by reference to past performance, of the future earning or dividend capacity of the company. He must understand business and business people, management and managers.

It is important to be satisfied that the assets of the company are all business assets which are necessary to generate the earnings of the company, and to identify any assets that are surplus to these requirements. The company's earnings must be capitalised by reference to an acceptable price-to-earnings ratio (5.4) or some other required yield (4.8; 5.6) — this is a matter that will exercise the valuer's skill and experience, and is often the arena for dispute between experts, for there are probably as many views on share valuation techniques as there are valuation experts. The company's dividend policy (or lack of it) must be investigated to see what the future can promise for shareholders in dividend terms (see 4.3).

If a hybrid basis (Chapter 7) is to be used, all or some of the factors — assets and surplus assets, earnings and

# Valuation checklist

☐ Client's name
☐ Company name
☐ Share capital
☐ Shareholders
☐ Shareholding to be valued
☐ Previous sales and transfers
☐ Relationship of client to company
☐ Relationship of client to shareholders
☐ Date for valuation
☐ Purpose of valuation
☐ Sources of information
☐ Subject company profile
☐ Basis of valuation
☐ Statutory rules
☐ Mem & Arts
☐ Resolutions and agreements
☐ Special rights, votes
☐ Financial and management background
☐ Flotation, takeover, liquidation likelihood
☐ Balance sheets and accounts
☐ Dividend policy
☐ Management projections and profit forecasts
☐ Directors and personnel
☐ Tax computations and liabilities
☐ Assets and real estate
☐ Liabilities
☐ Order book
☐ Suppliers, joint ventures and commitments
☐ Bad debts
☐ Exceptional, extraordinary expenditure
☐ Foreign trading and currency exposure
☐ Financial rates and data
☐ Future trading prospects
☐ General economic outlook
☐ Valuation approach (concepts reviewed) .
☐ Comparisons (quoted or other cos)
☐ Calculation
☐ Taxation
☐ Review

☐ Accounts
☐ Mem & Arts
☐ Resolutions & Minutes
☐ Material contracts
☐ Asset valuations
☐ Financial data
☐ Directors etc statements

dividends — may be given an individual weighting according to their perceived relative importance to the shareholding in question. The share valuation will be constructed from the duly weighted values by dividing the total value so determined by the number of shares in issue and multiplying by the shareholding being valued. This may then be discounted to reflect the problems of marketability (see 2.16) of the private company shares — including the problem of pre-emption rights and restrictions on transfer (see 2.13) normally written into a company's Articles of Association.

All the foregoing matters are considered in greater detail in the following Chapters of this book. A guide to the preparation of a valuation report is given in Chapter 9, and a sample valuation is given at the end of the book. The valuation checklist on page 9 broadly follows the arrangement of Chapter 9, the Share Valuation Report.

# Chapter 2

# Concepts in valuation

## 2.1 Background

As stated in Chapter 1, there are many occasions which give rise to a requirement to value private company shares and each occasion may require a slightly different approach, a different emphasis, or have regard to special factors.

A number of fundamental concepts in share valuation have sprung from or have been clarified by a range of judicial decisions and *dicta*. Most of the cases are concerned with valuations for tax purposes, notably estate duty, stamp duty and land duty; very few have been concerned with share valuation disputes. Many cases have concerned company law, compulsory acquisition, administration and negligence.

Because the tax statutes themselves are of minimal assistance in understanding valuation principles, the courts have had regard to common sense and practical interpretations with the result that the principles expounded by the courts in the tax cases often provide valuable assistance for other valuation purposes.

## 2.2 Open market value

For valuations of private company shares for fiscal purposes it is necessary to base the valuation on an assumed sale of the shares in the *open market* at the appropriate time (see Chapter 8). The concept of open market embraces the place of the market; the purchasers;

the willingness of both seller and purchaser to do a deal at a price; and the time of the transaction.

In *IRC* v *Clay*, Swinfen Eady LJ said:

> "The market is to be the open market, as distinguished from an offer to a limited class only, such as members of the family. The market is not necessarily an auction sale."

For non-fiscal valuations, the special factors that are drawn into a valuation by tax statutes — such as no discount for flooding the market, and information (see Chapter 8) — will be absent. However, it is likely that an "open market" valuation will be required, and it would certainly be wise to work on that basis unless some specific requirement dictates otherwise. For example, a transfer of shares between two parties under terms set out in, perhaps, the company's Articles of Association or other agreement, may require a "fair value" to be ascertained. "Fair value" is discussed below, and may be otherwise than "open market" value.

Whatever value is taken for any transfer, if there is likely to be a tax consequence then it is probable that an adjustment will be made to the value to ascertain the required open market value for tax purposes. An example may be the issue of new shares to an employee, where the Inland Revenue view of the open market value differs from the company's and the employee's views of the value of the shares. A compensating adjustment for tax purposes may be required (see 1.9 and 8.4).

## 2.3 Hypothetical open market

For tax purposes, at least, a hypothetical sale is assumed to take place in a hypothetical open market which includes any "special purchaser". In the case of *Re Lynall*, Plowman J said:

> "It is common ground that the shares must be valued on the basis of a hypothetical sale . . . in a hypothetical open market between a hypothetical willing vendor . . . and a hypothetical willing purchaser on the hypothesis that no-one is excluded from buying and that the

purchaser would be registered as the holder of his shares but would then hold them subject to the Articles of Association of the company, including the restrictions on transfer."

In *Re Holt*, Mr Justice Danckwerts uttered the following memorable lines:

"The result is that I must enter into a dim world peopled by the indeterminate spirits of fictitious or unborn sales. It is necessary to assume the prophetic vision of a prospective purchaser at the moment of the death of the deceased, and firmly to reject the wisdom which might be provided by the knowledge of subsequent events."

That case concerned estate duty, but the principle espoused is fundamental to any valuation requiring an open market basis.

In *Smyth* v *IRC*, Hannah J, rejecting the Revenue's restrictive contention that the most likely purchaser of shares (in this particular case) would be someone desiring a block of shares, said:

"In visualising the hypothetical open market I consider that it may contain some persons looking merely for a return of their money in a going concern, or some members of the family anxious to buy, and perhaps willing to give more than the ordinary buyer, in order to keep the business in the family, as well as the block purchaser, who wants to wind up the company for some reason, or to have a profit on his speculation."

Hannah J was emphasising the "openness" of the hypothetical market; see paragraph 2.5 below.

## 2.4 Willing buyer and seller

In the hypothetical market it has been considered necessary to have a hypothetical willing seller and hypothetical willing buyer. Harman LJ in *Re Lynall* explained that the willing vendor is a person who must sell and cannot simply call off the sale if he does not like the price; but on the other hand there must be a willing purchaser so that the conditions of the sale must be such as to induce in him a willing frame of mind. The willing seller was defined in *IRC* v *Buchanan* and distinguished from a sale which is made by reason of compulsory powers. Swinfen Eady LJ said:

> "It does not mean a sale by a person willing to sell his property without reserve for any price he can obtain". But he went on "she was willing to sell at a price she was offered, a price less than the maximum which the intending purchasers were willing to give, and she took it."

He held that she was a willing seller.

In *Buccleuch* v *IRC*, Lord Reid almost imputed a willingness on the seller when he said:

> "What must be envisaged is a sale in the open market on a particular day. So *there is no room* for supposing that the owner would do as many prudent owners do — withdraw the property if he does not get a sufficient offer and wait until a time when he can get a better offer."

The concept of a willing seller was introduced in the Finance (1909-1910) Act 1910 s.25(1) but the term is now found in fiscal legislation only in respect of the information that is made available to prospective purchasers by a "willing vendor" — see 2.6. Otherwise tax legislation simply assumes the sale to be in the open market at the relevant date.

If there is doubt whether the vendor is required actually to be "willing", there are two possible solutions. First, given that what is required is an "open market value", and for income tax, capital gains tax and capital transfer tax/ inheritance tax, what might *reasonably* be expected to be obtained" therefrom, it is almost inconceivable that any such open market would have an unwilling vendor present in it — it is therefore a consequence of the hypothetical open market rule that the vendor be hypothetically willing.

Alternatively, if the vendor is indeed unwilling, this would not in fact affect the open market value that would be obtained were the transaction to take place (which could only happen with a willing vendor). All the valuer is interested in is what that value would be. In the author's opinion, the omission of the words "willing vendor" from present tax valuation rules simply reflects the fact that the words are not required; the principle of a willing vendor is encompassed in the open market requirement.

In Finance (1909-10) Act 1910 s.25 the wording was rather loose: "The gross value of land means the amount which the fee simple of the land, if sold at the time in the open market by a willing seller . . . might be expected to realise".

Given the other open market value principles (considered in this Chapter), the value that is being sought is the best "reasonable" value that could be obtained — the degree of the vendor's "willingness" must unquestionably be regarded as allowing this value to be obtained or at least not obstructing its being obtained.

In *IRC* v *Clay* (on the meaning of "willing vendor" in relation to Finance (1909-10) Act 1910 s.25) Pickford LJ described the person as "one who is prepared to sell, provided a fair price is obtained — not an anxious seller". This seems to strike the right chord.

Whether or not the vendor is "willing", it is inconceivable that a purchaser would not be a willing purchaser — at the right price. Lord Fleming, in the case of *Findlay's Trustees* v *IRC*, describes the willing purchaser as a person of reasonable prudence, who has informed himself with regard to all the relevant facts such as the history of the business, its present position, its future prospects and the general conditions of the industry; and who also has access to the accounts of the business for a number of years. This cannot be taken too far — see 2.6 below.

## 2.5 Every possible purchaser

A number of cases have come before the courts on the matter of open market value. In the land value duty cases of *IRC* v *Buchanan*, Pickford LJ said that "a value ascertained by reference to the amount obtainable in an open market shows an intention to include every possible purchaser."

In *A-G* v *Jameson*, Fitzgibbon LJ said that one must look at "the price which would be obtainable upon a sale where it was open to everyone who had the will and the money, to offer the price which the property . . . was worth". Again, in *IRC* v *Buchanan*, Swinfen Eady LJ said that "the market is to be the open market, as distinguished from an offer to a limited class only . . . The market is not necessarily an auction sale."

In the estate duty case of *Duke of Buccleuch* v *IRC* Lord Reed, discussing the proposition that the sale takes place *in the open market*, expressed his view that "the phrase requires that the seller must take such steps as are reasonable to attract as much competition as possible for the particular piece of property which is to be sold. Sometimes this will be by sale by auction, sometimes otherwise." See also 2.11.


## 2.6 Available information

*General*

"The sum which any bidder will offer must depend on what he knows (or thinks he knows) about the property for which he bids." (Lord Reid in *Re Lynall*).

It has to be assumed that information is available to our hypothetical purchasers. In *Re Lynall*, Lord Morris of Borth-y-Gest, in considering what information could be available to hypothetical purchasers and vendors in the open market said:

> "this must mean whether it would be openly available to all potential purchasers and vendors in the market or markets in which relevant purchases and sales take place. There may be different markets or types of markets for different varieties of property, but . . . the market which must be contemplated, whatever its form, must be an "open" market in which the property

is offered for sale to the world at large so that all potential purchasers have an equal opportunity to make an offer as a result of it being openly known what it is that is being offered for sale. Mere private deals on a confidential basis are not the equivalent of open market transactions."

However, in valuing shares for capital gains tax or capital transfer tax purposes the legislation states:

"it shall be assumed that in the open market which is postulated . . . there is available to any prospective purchaser of the asset in question all the information which a prudent prospective purchaser of the asset might reasonably require *if he were proposing to purchase it from a willing vendor by private treaty and at arm's length*" (Capital Gains Tax Act 1979 s.152(2));

and

"In determining the price which unquoted shares or securities might reasonably be expected to fetch if sold in the open market it shall be assumed that in that market there is available to any prospective purchaser of the shares or securities all the information which a prudent prospective purchaser might reasonably require *if he were proposing to purchase them from a willing vendor by private treaty and at arm's length*" (Capital Transfer Tax Act 1984, s.168(1)).

Thus, Lord Morris's dismissal of "mere private deals" cannot now be relied upon for capital gains tax and capital transfer tax/inheritance tax valuation purposes, but may still be applicable in other circumstances.

## *"Reasonable" directors*

In relation to the question of how far information concerning the value of shares could be made public, Lord Reid in the *Re Lynall* case said:

"The furthest we could possibly go would be to hold that the directors must be deemed to have done what all *reasonable directors* would do. Then it might be reasonable to say that they would disclose information provided that its disclosure could not possibly prejudice the interests of the company."

Interestingly, he went on:

> "Not all financiers who might wish to bid in such a sale, and not even all accountants whom they might nominate, are equally trustworthy . . . I could not hold it right to suppose that all reasonable directors would agree to disclose information such as these reports [being reports which made it very probable that a public issue would be made in the near future] so widely as would be necessary if it had to be made available to all who must be regarded as genuine potential bidders or their nominees."

In a private treaty sale for a majority interest it is probable that such information would be divulged; not necessarily however, or perhaps particularly not, in the case of a minority sale.

In a major acquisition of shares it is usual for the purchaser to require that the company's books and records be made available to his accountants for confidential scrutiny. How much information would be allowed to be divulged by "reasonable" directors would largely depend upon the size or importance of the share acquisition. The amount of information that "reasonable directors" would divulge in a disposal of a minority interest would probably be less than in a subscription for new shares. Indeed the directors may see no good reason at all for disclosing any confidential information to minority shareholders.

The sale of shares to a director was considered in the case of *Percival* v *Wright* and it was held that the purchasing directors were under no obligation to disclose to their vendor shareholders matters which are "merely incidents in the ordinary course of management". Such matters included large casual profits, the discovery of a new vein (it was a colliery company), good prospective dividends, and negotiations for a sale of the company undertaking. Equally, a director selling shares is under no obligation to disclose losses.

In general, a director is under no legal obligation to make confidential information available; indeed no director should disclose confidential information without the consent of the board of directors.

18

## Memorandum and Articles of Association and minute book

Information not available to a prospective purchaser will be available to the valuer, who would commence his valuation exercise by an examination of the company's Memorandum and Articles of Association; the company's minute book might also be inspected. Under the Companies Act 1985 s.383, the minute book must be kept available for inspection by members, but not by the general public. Therefore, although the valuer might inspect it for evidence of proper conduct of statutory duties and any other relevant matters, the information in the minute book would not normally be available to a prospective purchaser (other than possibly a majority shareholder) prior to an acquisition. Confidential information, which, if known to the purchaser, might affect the value of the company's shares should not necessarily be adopted as a factor affecting that value unless it is reasonable to assume that the information would be made available to that purchaser on the principles discussed above.

The company's Memorandum and Articles of Association, register of directors and secretary, register of mortgages and charges, annual return and accounts, or modified accounts, are all available for public inspection at Companies House. Any prospective purchaser of shares would probably carry out a company search as the first stage and so would know the full entitlements and rights attaching to the shares. This course of action should be followed whether the acquisition is from an existing shareholder, or is of an issue of new shares by the company.

## Warranties and indemnities

Additionally, the purchaser of a majority interest would probably require warranties from the present directors and possibly also from the shareholders (especially if they were involved in the management of the company).

The warranties that might attach to a share sale agree-

19

ment relate to liabilities in respect of matters such as taxation, property and fixed assets, company law, trading and profit and loss account, finance, employment, trading activities and contracts. A full set of warranties can be most intimidating and much time can be spent simply negotiating which warranties will remain and which will be left out — the vendor wishing for none; the purchaser requiring all. The valuer should therefore consider:

(a) whether the acquisition is one in which warranties and indemnities would be required, and given; and

(b) if so, whether the discovery of confidential information after the sale would give cause for an action by the purchaser under the terms of the sale contract, either for rescission or, more likely, for damages, and whether a liability would be likely to be incurred because of the indemnity given by the shareholders.

So, any adverse facts that it would be reasonable to expect would be covered by warranties should not be ignored in a valuation. Equally, the fact that no-one would give warranties to the purchaser of a minority interest might be considered to be a discounting factor. Even if a shareholder gave general warranties, unless it could clearly be established that he had access to adverse facts that were known to the directors of the company it would be difficult to take action against him unless, unwisely from the vendor's point of view, the warranties were of a specific and categoric nature. No mere shareholder would give such warranties.

## 2.7 Transferee standing in shoes of transferor

In *Stanyforth* v *IRC* Lord Warrington of Cliff said that the property for sale in an open market:

> "would have to be put up with all its incidents, including provisions for defeasance either in whole or in part, powers vested in persons not controlled by the vendor to create charges taking precedence of the property sold, and so forth."

Thus, where a power to affect the value of any property adversely or to destroy it vests in some person over whom the purchaser has no control, this "incident" of the property cannot be disregarded. In the context of company shares, existing options, restrictions on transfers (see 2.13) and the like are relevant.

The transferee must stand in the shoes of the transferor. Chief Baron Palles in *A-G* v *Jameson* said that the hypothetical sale and purchase must be of the entire legal and equitable interest therein, of that interest by virtue of which the transferor was entitled to be a member of the company in respect of the shares; it must be a sale whereby the purchaser would be entitled to have that which he has bought vested in him in the same manner as it had been vested in the (hypothetical) seller, and consequently under which he would be entitled to be registered as a member of the company in respect of those shares; and this assumption must be made whilst excluding from consideration any provisions in the Articles of Association as actually do prevent a purchaser at the time of the sale from becoming a member of the company and registered as such in respect of the shares.

In the same case, Walker LJ said that the test of value (for estate duty purposes) is what the shares would fetch if sold in open market — a hypothetical open market — upon the terms that the purchaser would be entitled to be registered in respect of the shares but would himself thereafter hold them subject to the provisions of the Articles of Association, including those relating to alienation and transfer. This price he said, was not limited to the "fair value" (see 2.10 below).

This matter is more exhaustively dealt with in 2.13 below.

## 2.8 Date for valuation

The date upon which the valuation is required should be regarded as a frozen point in time which cannot be influenced by events which have not yet taken place, even though at the time of the valuation exercise there is knowledge of sales, transactions or influential events subsequent to the valuation date; this applies certainly for fiscal purposes and usually for other purposes (but see 2.10).

Lord Morris of Borth-y-Gest in the estate duty case of *Duke of Buccleuch* v *IRC* said:

> "the value of any property must be estimated to be the price which, in the opinion of the Commissioners, the property would fetch if sold in the open market at the time of the death of the deceased. 'At the time of death' must not be paraphrased or altered so as to read 'within a reasonably short time of the death'. It follows from this that the section is envisaging a hypothetical sale at the time of death. This is quite inconsistent with a notion that the value of a piece of property is to be estimated by postulating that preparations for an actual sale would be commenced at but after the time of death and that a sale would later follow after such preparation."

In that case, the taxpayer contended that a landed estate which was inherited could not possibly be sold at the time of death but would take several years to dispose of.

Lord Reed in the *Duke of Buccleuch* case said that as the valuation was required for a particular time (ie the date of death of the taxpayer):

> "There was no room for supposing that the owner would do as many prudent owners do — withdraw the property if he does not get a sufficient offer and wait until a time when he can get a better offer. The Commissioners must estimate what the property would probably have fetched on that particular day if it had then been exposed for sale, no doubt after such advance publicity as would have been reasonable."

The value of some assets can be particularly susceptible to cyclical or seasonal fluctuations. Residential property, for example, may be more easily sold or may command a higher price in the spring and summer months than in autumn and winter.

In the case of *IRC* v *Marr's Trustees*, a herd of cattle was considered, and for valuation purposes the definite ascertainable condition of the herd at the valuation date and at no later time was taken. "At that date a cow may be two or three weeks from calving. In the course of three or four months, the risks of calving and the risks to the life of the young calf are largely over: the two conditions are completely different things."

See also 2.15.

## 2.9 The price the property would fetch

No allowance for notional expenses on the notional disposal can be taken for fiscal valuation purposes. In the *Buccleuch* case, Lord Guest said that the 'price the property would fetch' (in Finance Act 1894 s.7(5)) means not the price which the vendor would have received but what the purchaser would have paid to be put into the shoes of the deceased. He went on to say that this means that the cost of realisation does not form a legitimate deduction in arriving at the valuation. Indeed, he said, in s.7(3) a specific deduction of 5% was allowed in arriving at the value of foreign property for estate duty and this only emphasised the fact that no costs of realisation are permissible deductions in arriving at the valuation of properties within the UK for fiscal purposes. In the Capital Gains Tax Act 1979 s.150(5), in relation to assets subject to exchange control restrictions in the UK, the "market value" for capital gains tax purposes is "subject to such adjustment as is appropriate having regard to the difference between the amount payable by a purchaser and the amount receivable by a seller". Those would appear to be the only circumstances allowing a deduction to acknowledge the fact that the eventual net receipt by the vendor is usually less than the market value. The 5% deduction for estate duty purposes is not statutorily available for foreign property under the capital transfer tax/inheritance tax regime.

However, nothing was said by Lord Guest about the costs of the purchaser — professional fees and stamp duty for example — although these considerations are more likely to be relevant to assets other than shares.

In the case of *Earl of Ellesmere* v *IRC*, Sankey J pointed out that a sale in the open market does not necessarily mean the price which would be fetched upon a sale to a single purchaser. He cited the case of an owner having property including a colliery and a draper's shop, suggesting that if the colliery and the draper's shop were sold separately the best possible price might be obtained for each. On the other hand, a purchaser who was anxious to buy the draper's shop might not wish to be encumbered with the colliery and *vice versa*. What is meant by the words "the price which it would fetch if sold in the open market" was the best possible price that is obtainable and that is largely, if not entirely, a question of fact.

Lord Reed in the *Duke of Buccleuch* case, tempered this by explaining how, if applied as a universal rule, it would create enormous difficulties. He cited the case of the owner of a wholesale business who dies possessed of a large quantity of merchandise. It would have been possible by extensive advertising to obtain offers for small lots of something near retail prices and thereby realise the stock at much more than wholesale prices. It may not have been reasonable and it may not have been economic but it would have been possible. He said that "there is no universal rule that the best possible prices at the date of death must be taken." The principle of dividing up the assets is not so much directed at a disposal of shares as at separate assets but, theoretically, there may be instances where a break-up of a single shareholding or a combination of different classes of share would bring this principle into play.

The case of *A-G of Ceylon* v *Mackie* considered the situation where a better price was obtained by aggregating shareholdings than by sub-dividing them. In that case, it was clearly established that a higher price would be got on a sale of the combined holding of ordinary and preference shares because of restrictions in the Articles of Association which made a sale of any of the shares in isolation untenable from an investment point of view.

## 2.10 Fair value (and other expressions of value)

Often, a company's Articles of Association include provision for transfers of the company's shares to be made at a "fair value". The situation usually envisaged is a transfer under the pre-emption article from an existing registered shareholder to another such shareholder or possibly a transfer by virtue of an employee shareholder leaving employment. Sometimes, sale agreements, options and other private commercial arrangements may also call for a "fair value" instead of an "open market" value.

In these cases the quantification of the value is usually left to the company's auditors or some other independent party and usually that party is required to act as an expert, not an arbitrator.

In fact, the expressions that may be used include "full value", "market value", "open market value", "fair market value", "fair open market value", "fair value", "arm's length value" or even "par value" or "nominal value". Dealing with the last two first, ascertaining the par or nominal value of shares should not be difficult as such. There may be other problems arising, however, because in such a case a transfer may be taking place at a considerable under-value for tax purposes. Wherever transfers are required to be made at such value care should be taken to ascertain the full facts relating to the agreement and the reasoning behind the transfer. Par value or nominal value cannot be taken for share valuation purposes if the "worth" or market value of the shares is different (*McIlquham* v *Taylor* and see also 2.13).

The fact that shares can only be transferred at a fixed or nominal value or by reference to a closed market, will not prevent an open market value being required for tax valuation purposes, although such restrictions may in some cases have an impact on the open market value — see 2.13. The use of the word "fair" with "market value" or "open market value" can only be taken to be an unnecessary embellishment, but does "fair value" differ from "open market value"?

Some assistance can be found in the ordinary dictionary

meaning. The first definition of the word "fair" (as a noun) in the *Shorter Oxford Dictionary* is: "A periodical gathering of buyers and sellers, in a place and at a time ordained by charter or statute or by ancient custom". On that basis fair value would surely be no different from, and indeed would in fact be, open market value. But the usage of the word suggests another dictionary definition: "Free from bias, fraud or injustice; equitable, legitimate". How then is this definition different, if at all, from "open market value"? Further assistance can be found in Walker LJ's comment in *A-G* v *Jameson* that an open market price was not limited to the fair value; see 2.7.

In determining a fair value, it must be presumed that the value must be as fair *as between the parties*, and this must be the crux of the matter. One is not being asked to take the open, or indeed, a closed market value; or to take a tax value or a compulsory purchase value; or to take the side of the vendor or of the purchaser. What one is being asked to do is to examine the extremes of value that either party might argue for himself and then, looking at all the circumstances, even-handedly determine where, within that range of values, a value that reflects those circumstances fairly as between the parties can be found.

Open market price is certainly a starting point, but, for example, it may be decided that "special purchaser" considerations should not be introduced because the shares in question cannot in reality hope to find themselves available in the open market. Against this, excessive restrictions in the Articles of Association on the transfer of shares may artificially depress the value of a share and it may be thought right that these restrictions be discounted in seeking a fair value; on the other hand if the acquirer cannot turn his newly acquired shares to account because those same restrictions now apply to him and he cannot alter them, the valuer may regard those restrictions as having the opposite effect on the value. If the acquiror of a minority shareholding thereby becomes a majority shareholder and able to deal freely with the shares, while before the transfer he could not, it may be considered that a fair price would be something above the minority value, but not so that it becomes a hostage value. Indeed, a fair value may well be considered to be a value that is not discounted to the same extent as open market value minority shareholdings.

A fair value may also take more account of pre- and post-valuation day events than open market value principles for tax purposes allow, unless it seems unfair to one of the parties to do so.

The fair value approach cannot ignore the circumstances surrounding the valuation; it can ignore some of the extremes that may be associated with an open market value but its principal purpose is usually to reduce bargaining and avoid hostage values. It certainly does not mean that the fundamental valuation bases can be ignored; having said that, one or two cases have supported, in special circumstances, a valuation of minority interests on a *pro rata* basis. These cases are mentioned below.

As already mentioned (see 1.2) the valuer is asked to act as expert not arbitrator and as expert he can find himself open to an action for negligence. Usually, his "opinion" on the matter will be final, but this will obviously depend on the wording of the agreement or Articles.

In *Dean* v *Prince* Denning LJ said:

> "Suppose it had been Mr Prince who had died, leaving only thirty shares. Those thirty shares, being a minority holding, would fetch nothing in the open market. But does that mean that the other directors would be entitled to take his shares for nothing? Surely not. No matter which director it was who happened to die his widow should be entitled to the same price per share, irrespective of whether her husband's holding was large or small. It seems to me that the fair thing to do would be to take the whole two hundred shares of the company and see what they were worth, and then pay the widow a sum appropriate to her husband's holding. At any rate if the auditor was of the opinion that that was a fair method, no-one can say that he was wrong."

In connection with the special purchaser concept (see 2.11 below) he said:

"I am prepared to concede that the shares might realise an enhanced value on that account, but I do not think it would be a fair price to ask the directors to pay. They were buying these shares — under a compulsory sale and purchase — on the assumption that they would continue in the business as working directors. It would be unfair to make them pay a price based on the assumption that they would be turned out (of their own factory). If the auditor never took that possibility into account, he cannot be blamed for he was only asked to certify the fair value of the shares. The only fair value would be to take a hypothetical purchaser who was prepared to carry on the business if it was worth while so to do, or otherwise to put it into liquidation. At any rate if that was the auditor's opinion, no-one can say he was wrong."

Denning's thoughts in relation to a *pro rata* valuation were echoed by Mr Justice Nourse in *Re Company No 003420* (a case concerning oppression of minority interests — see 2.14), where he said:

"In the majority of cases of purchase orders under section 75 (Companies Act 1980 — but see now Companies Act 1985 s.461(2)(d)) the vendor would be unwilling in the sense that the sale would have been forced upon him. He would usually be a minority shareholder whose interests had been unfairly prejudiced by the manner in which the majority had conducted the company's affairs.

On the assumption that unfair prejudice had made it intolerable for him to retain his interest in the company, a sale would invariably be the only practical way out, short of winding-up. In such a case it would not merely not be fair, but most unfair, that he should be bought out on the fictional basis applicable to a free election to sell his shares in accordance with the company's Articles of Association, or on any other basis which involved a discounted price.

The correct course would be to fix the price pro rata according to the value of the company's shares as a whole, as being the only fair method of compensating an unwilling vendor of the equivalent of a partnership share.

Equally, if the order provided for the purchase of the

shares of the delinquent majority, it would not receive a price which involved an element of premium."

Thus a *pro rata* basis may be worth considering in determining the fair value of the shares, but the only technical support the valuer would have in choosing such a basis would be in cases of oppression of minorities (see 2.14); in companies that could be described as quasi-partnerships; and Denning's view (above) that an auditor's opinion that that basis was a fair basis could not be said to be wrong.

## 2.11 Special purchaser

*General*

In viewing the hypothetical open market the valuer must consider whether the existence of a "special purchaser" in that market would affect the price obtainable for the property (whether shares or other assets). The special purchaser is a person for whom the property for sale would have a greater value than it has for anyone else in the market, although it is not necessary to suppose that he would definitely be in the market at the time of valuation.

A number of cases have considered such a purchaser, and the main principle that has emerged is that if the existence of the special purchaser in the market place is or would be known at the date for the valuation the price of the property may be greater than it would be otherwise; if the existence of such a special purchaser is not known then, whether or not there actually might be one, the price would not be affected.

The special purchaser must be an identified person (or possibly class of person) and must be in a special position in relation to the property in question. It is not correct to postulate a special purchaser. The open market is just that — open.

*Intermediary purchaser*

In certain cases involving land, it has been held that the

circumstances or value of surrounding land should not be ignored. In the land value duty case of *IRC* v *Buchanan*, for example, Cozens-Hardy MR said that:

> "to say that a small farm in the middle of a wealthy landowner's estate is to be valued without reference to the fact that he will probably be willing to pay a large price, seems to me to be absurd. If the landowner does not at that moment buy, landbrokers and speculators will give more than its pure agricultural value with a view to re-selling it at a profit to the landowner."

In the case of *Raja Vyricherla Narayana Gajapatiraju* v *RDO, Vizagapatam*, which was an Indian compulsory purchase case heard by the Privy Council, Lord Romer said that it has been established by numerous authorities that land is not valued merely by reference to the use to which it is being put at the time at which its value has to be determined, but also by reference to the uses to which it is reasonably capable of being put in the future.

Also, in the *Buchanan* case, Swinfen Eady LJ suggested that the knowledge that a special purchaser was interested would affect the market price of the property and other potential purchasers would join in competing for it with a view to obtaining it at a price less than that which they believe the special purchaser would pay. To ascertain how the open market value is actually affected by this, is the price the special purchaser would pay to be taken and then discounted by a "dealing" profit, or should the ordinary open market price be used and increased by an amount beyond which the intermediary purchaser would not go for fear of not making his profit on the deal?

It has already been said that if the existence of a special purchaser in the market is not known to other bidders, his existence cannot affect the value of the shares. This is because the unknown special purchaser would need only to make an additional bid above the normal buyer to clinch the deal, and perhaps the additional bid would in fact be no more than £1 or an offer to meet legal costs of both parties. So the additional bid is unlikely to be material in relation to the maximum open market price. It may be suggested that if this additional bid were made in public (ie at an auction) it might have the effect of putting up the market value; but there is no reason to suppose that the shares would be bid for at auction. An auction sale is not a required element in valuation; but it will take its proper place in the open market. Thus, we can assume an auction market where it is usual and appropriate to do so (see *IRC* v *Buchanan* and 2.5).

It is also true that even if the existence of a special purchaser is known the ordinary market value may not be materially affected. First, the maximum price he is prepared to pay may be impossible to determine and therefore the speculator wishing to take advantage of the special purchaser would be in a considerable dilemma. It does not seem at all reasonable to suppose that bull-headed speculators are in the open market, and indeed such types appear more properly to fall into the category of special purchaser with personal reasons for investing (dealt with below). The dilemma would arise out of knowing that some profit can be made but not knowing how much and therefore not being able to quantify the risk attaching to a speculative buy. The speculator would only buy the shares if he was confident of being able to sell on at a profit. Indeed, the special purchaser can only have a marked effect on the open market value if the intermediary purchaser will be able to sell on to that special purchaser at a profit.

Two other reasons why the share price might not be affected even though a special purchaser is known to exist and that a profit, whether or not determinable, could be made, are first, the uncertainty of selling on the shares to the special purchaser within a reasonable period of time, loss of interest, for example, on the money invested may be relevant (but may be answered by company earnings or dividends).

Secondly, in relation to minority interests, restrictions on transfer of shares may make it unattractive to the speculator to become involved. The fact that shares cannot be transferred or registered in the name of any new shareholder because of restrictions in the Articles of Association does not prevent them being "deemed" to be transferred for valuation purposes and thereafter held subject to those restrictions (see 2.13). However, it may be difficult to apply this "deeming" rule to a speculator. Following the *Re Lynall* decision, where it was said that the hypothetical purchaser was deemed to be registered as a shareholder and would thereafter hold the shares subject to the company's Memorandum and Articles of Association, if the Articles of Association carried restrictions on transfer by the new shareholder, the speculator as that new shareholder would be unable to realise his profit. Therefore, although it may be acceptable to apply the deeming rule as between a willing buyer and seller in a hypothetical market it must be questionable to assume that a hypothetical intermediary as a speculator would acquire shares that are subject to restrictions on transfer.

In *Re Lynall* Widgery LJ said:

> "It is desirable, in my opinion, that when the Court is constructing the conditions under which the hypothetical sale is deemed to take place it should build upon a foundation of reality, so far as this is possible, but it is even more important that it should not defeat the intention of the section (Finance Act 1984 s.7(5)) by an undue concern for reality in what is essentially a hypothetical situation. In the case of speculations, it seems to be necessary to look at the reality of the case — ie the speculator could not in fact as a practical proposition enter into the hypothetical market place."

However, knowing of the existence of the special purchaser, the vendor might himself be able to negotiate directly a price higher than would otherwise be offered, but less than that required to be paid to an intermediary. Timing may be important, depending on whether or not the special purchaser is in the market for *immediate* purchase.

But even in this case some knowledge of what the special purchaser would pay is necessary and this must be more than pure guesswork. If no value can be estimated on genuine grounds then there is little basis for supposing that the ordinary market value can be increased at all or at best by more than a notional amount.

There need not be only one special purchaser in the market; there may well be more. If so, presumably the value of the shares for sale will increase because of the possibility of the special purchasers bidding against each other. It is not correct to theorise; it is a question of fact, and therefore evidence, as to whether there is one, two or a hundred special purchasers in the market.

Of course, the more special purchasers there are the less "special" they become; the more they become part of the ordinary open market, and the more likely it is that the price each is prepared to pay is known.

## Personal factors

Lord Johnston in *IRC* v *Marrs Trustees* held that if the special purchaser's price is based on factors personal to himself that price should not prevail for valuation purposes. The facts in that case were that a bidder was able to increase his bid for cattle wholly because he had found an underwriter who was prepared to insure certain related risk in ignorance of the normal insurance practice relating to such cattle risk.

But there is a distinction between personal factors and self-evident potential for an increase in the value of the asset being sold. In the case of *Robinson Bros (Brewers) Ltd* v *Houghton and Chester-le-Street Assessment Committee*, Lord MacMillan said: "the motives which activate buyers in a market may be of all kinds, but it is not their motives, but their bids, that matter."

This case concerned the rating valuation of a public house and the question arose whether the fact that brewers would pay a higher rent for managed houses was a factor that should be taken into account in the rating valuation. Lord MacMillan went on, referring to the brewer:

> "why should the rent which he is prepared to pay be excluded from consideration in fixing the market value of the tenancy? He is one of the competitors in the market and the figure which he is prepared to pay is an element which ought clearly to be taken into account in arriving at the market price."

In *IRC* v *Crossman*, the Lord Chancellor gave his opinion that the right way in which to arrive at the value in the open market was not to exclude or include anybody in particular but to consider the matter generally. On evidence that a special purchaser was prepared to pay a much higher price than could otherwise be found because of certain particular attractions for the special purchaser, the Lord Chancellor held that the extra sum which could be obtained from that special purchaser was not an element of value in the open market but rather a particular price beyond the ordinary market price, which the special purchaser in this case would give for special reasons of his own.

In *Re Lynall*, a case concerning a close family-owned and run company, it was held that a director who would give an enhanced price because he would thus obtain control of the company would be left out of account because he had a special personal reason for paying that price. But on the other hand that did not preclude directors as such from being in the market place.

The *Re Lynall* decision is important because it implies that the valuation of a minority interest in a family company would not be inflated by the existence of another family member/director who might wish to acquire the minority interest and thus obtain control, except (as is unlikely) to the extent that his *active* presence in the market would be known to other potential purchasers who might increase their bids accordingly. In the author's opinion the mere fact that a minority shareholder could become a majority shareholder if he acquired the shares that are for sale does not amount to public knowledge about the existence of a special purchaser.

## 2.12 Special markets

In the vast majority of private company share valuations a comparison with quoted companies in a similar sector involves so many variable factors that it is at best only a rough and ready guide, and at worst positively misleading. However, the possibility of a public flotation has been considered in *Re Lynall* and in *Re Holt*, and there may be some support for a closer comparison between the company whose shares are being valued and quoted companies.

The concept of a special *market* rather than a special *purchaser* has not been considered by the courts. However, in recent years, the possibility of a "special market" for shares has become clearer with the growing "over the counter" trade in shares and more especially because of the unlisted securities market. In both cases, there are costly and time-consuming pre-flotation procedures, and one of many reasons may prevent a planned flotation at the last minute. The general economic outlook at the time of flotation may depress the market for new issues. A major problem with a USM launch is that the striking price for the shares can rarely be confirmed until immediately before the flotation, when the whole exercise is highly charged with risk. It must also be remembered that the USM carries a far greater element of risk than the listed market, and, for example, Price to Earnings Ratios may change much more quickly.

The valuer should bear in mind that what is being valued is the shares in the shareholder's hands for sale at the date of valuation, and not a new issue of shares or a flotation. Over-sophistication is to be avoided.

## 2.13 Restrictions on transfer

The Articles of Association may carry restrictions on the transfer of shares, pre-emption clauses, valuation formulae and so on, each of which may affect the transferability of the shares.

In *IRC* v *Crossman*, Lord Russell of Killowen said:

> "It may be that owing to provisions in the articles ... the subject matter of the sale (the shares) cannot be effectively vested in the purchaser, because the directors refuse to and cannot be compelled to register the purchaser as shareholder. The purchaser could then secure the benefit of the sale by the registered shareholder becoming a trustee for him of the rights with an indemnity in respect of the obligations."

This illustrates that there is no bar to a valuation of shares, even though there may be a technicality that would prevent the clean-cut transfer of title. Having said that, if such a bar were burdensome on the acquirer of shares, one could see a reason for a discount from the value to reflect that burden.

In the estate duty case of *The Trustees of Johan Thomas Salvesen* v *IRC*, a company's Articles of Association, after allowing transfers of shares between members of the family, provided that "no share shall be transferred to any person who is not a member of the company so long as any member is willing to purchase the same at its nominal value if fully paid or at a price corresponding to the amount paid up on the same . . . " The Articles also provided that by extraordinary resolution the company could resolve that any shareholder, other than one holding more than 10% of the shares and other than directors could be required to transfer his shares. Lord Fleming said that these restrictions were onerous and would depreciate the value of the shares, but that did not necessarily mean the value would be as low as the nominal value contained in the Articles of Association.

In the case of *A-G* v *Jameson* the question was raised whether a fair value of a share which was set at a figure by the Articles of Association could be said to override the value which, in the opinion of the Commissioners, the property would fetch if sold in the open market at the time of death of the deceased (Finance Act 1984 s.7(5)). The consequences of fixing a fair value in the Articles was that none but members of the Jameson family would be shareholders of the company. The fair value was low enough to render unlikely any disposal of shares to prospective purchasers outside the family. Lord Ashbourne could not altogether ignore the fair value established in the Articles. He said:

> "The argument of the Attorney-General, which seeks to brush aside the articles and to vest in the executors a property which Henry Jameson never possessed, would ascribe to the Finance Act the power of making a new subject matter. The argument of the defendants clings

desperately to the Articles, and gives really no adequate signficance to the words of the Act requiring the Commissioners to estimate the price which the shares would fetch in the open market. The solution lies between the two. The Attorney-General must give more weight to the Articles, and the defendants to the statute. It requires no tremendous imagination to conceive what a purchaser would give in the open market for Henry Jameson's shares as Henry Jameson himself held them at his death — *for the right to stand in his shoes."*

Lord Ashbourne felt that although not so valuable as owning shares absolutely free and unfettered, the shares were worth more than the value attributed by the Articles and he could see no overwhelming difficulty in estimating the price they would fetch if sold in the open market.

An interesting point was made by Fitzgibbon LJ in the same case, where he said that the pre-emption clauses could be both appreciatory and depreciatory. Although the right of pre-emption against Henry Jameson's shares was a depreciating incident, the corresponding right (of Henry Jameson or any other person standing in his shoes) to acquire shares from other members at the fair value was an appreciating incident. However, in extending this argument, one might say that the appreciating incident arose simply out of being a shareholder, whether of one share or a large number of shares. See also 2.16.

## 2.14 Oppression of minorities

In valuing shares and, in particular, in looking at the rights and expectations of shareholders, the fact that one or more of the shareholders has a dominant power over the others cannot be manipulated so as to remove all rights of minority shareholders. The Companies Act 1985 ss.459-461 contains provisions to safeguard the minority shareholders' rights, and thus preserve the value of such shareholdings.

If shareholders who have a dominant power in a company exercise or threaten to exercise that power to procure that something is done or not done in the conduct of the company's affairs, and when that conduct is unfair or, in the words of Viscount Simonds in *Scottish Co-operative Wholesale Society Ltd* v *Meyer*, "burdensome, harsh and wrongful" to the minority shareholders and "lacks that degree of probity which they are entitled to expect in the conduct of the company's affairs", that action may be regarded as oppressive to the minority shareholders. They would then be entitled to petition the court for an appropriate order, for example, to regulate the company's affairs; enforce or prevent some act; authorise civil proceedings; enforce purchase of shares from a member of the company by other members or by the company itself (with subsequent reduction of capital). In such a case the court may in effect vary or override the Memorandum or Articles of the company; or may put the company into compulsory liquidation.

This applies to *wrongful* acts. It would not be oppression if, for example, the company refuses to buy out minority shareholdings. On the other hand, a planned campaign to divert the business of a company into another business medium under different control probably would be an oppression of minorities that might be remedied by the court requiring the wrong-doer to purchase the company's shares from the innocent parties.

In *Re Company Number 003420*, a case concerning an order under the Companies Act 1980 s.75 (now Companies Act 1985 s.461(2)(d)) for the majority shareholders to acquire the minority shareholders' shares, the company was held to fall into the category of a "quasi-partnership", ie the company had been incorporated to be the vehicle for the conduct of a business carried on by two or more shareholders which they could have carried on in partnership together. In such a case, where a shareholder had been unfairly prejudiced resulting in his exclusion from participating in the company's affairs, and he had not acted to justify that exclusion, the price of his shares should be fixed *pro rata* according to the value of the company's shares *as a whole* and not on the basis of a discounted minority interest (see Chapter 4).

The elements of a quasi-partnership and the application of the "just and equitable' rule for the making of an order for compulsory winding-up are discussed in *Ebrahimi* v *Westbourne Galleries Ltd.*

In *Re Company No 003420*, the *pro rata* valuation basis applied because it was the most fair in all the circumstances. In other circumstances perhaps a different "fair value" basis (see 2.10) would have been adopted, and if there had not been oppression of a minority interest in the first place, it is unlikely that the *pro rata* basis would have been used at all (see *Re Company Number 004475*).

## 2.15 Actual sales

*Present sales*

If an offer has been made for the company as a whole then it is highly unlikely, although not impossible, that the shareholders would sell for less than the bid price. However, it is incumbent upon the valuer to satisfy himself first, that the offer is genuine and from an independent third party, and secondly, that it is not, for example, an artificially low price based on the personal knowledge that the vendor is in extreme need of cash and in an untenable negotiating position, perhaps because of clawing creditors. If upon inspection the offer is *bona fide*, it is suggested that that bid price must constitute the company's value unless some material disparity can be identified through any of the other bases.

*Prior sales*

The case of *McNamee* v *RC*, an Irish estate duty case, may be quoted as authority for prior arm's length sales influencing the value of the shares. There may well be a case for having regard to a prior sale, of course, but care must be taken that it was a sale in a "real or imaginary open market", and also that it concerned a sale of shares in similar amounts and circumstances to those that are the subject of the current valuation. Further, the longer the time that has elapsed between the prior sale and the current valuation, the more difficult it is to say that the one is an influence on or indicative of the other. While the *McNamee* case clearly indicates that the court can be influenced by evidence of a recent arm's length sale, a careful reading also shows that the more clear evidence there is to support the present valuation, the more likely it is that the court will accept it.

Some authorities suggest that prior sales can actually be introduced into a hybrid valuation and weighted accordingly. It is suggested that, except where there are regular dealings in the shares such as to constitute a current market, this has the effect of distorting the current share value without contributing in real terms to any underlying value. Where a prior sale might be used to influence a share price is in determining any discounts or price to earnings ratio, but great care must be taken, and the full facts surrounding the prior sale must be ascertained. For example, the prior sale may have been entirely at arm's length, but the vendor may have been in exceptional personal need of cash and decided to sell off some of his shares at a bargain price (perhaps to a colleague) to put himself into funds. It is argued that this situation equates with the special purchaser who has personal reasons for investing (see 2.11) and so this sale value may be ignored for determining a current market value.

Subsequently, a vendor might transfer shares into a trust, possibly contemplating a flotation of his company. He might like to think that his trust shares would equate in value with what he accepted on an earlier sale, but in reality the value on the flotation could be considerably more than the first and bear no relationship to it. The other side of the coin might be that the company simply is no longer as valuable as it was — for whatever reason — and no previous sale can change that. Another case is where 100% of the shares of a company are bought and shortly afterwards a small proportion given to employees of the company. The first transaction (a 100% acquisition valued on prospects prior to acquisition) is likely to be valued on an entirely different basis from the interest given to employees.

*Subsequent sales*

The important practical point here is that if there is a sale shortly following the date of valuation, at a price different from the value given, and the matter is still in dispute with Shares Valuation Division, the sale price on the second transaction (again, if it relates to a similar number of shares in similar circumstances) must have a considerable bearing on the outcome of any negotiated agreement. Following the case of *IRC* v *Marr's Trustees*, however, the mere fact that a higher price could be had if the sale were delayed until better market conditions existed, should not of itself influence the value of the asset at the date for which valuation is required. However, on the special purchaser principle and in relation to controlling interests greater than 75%, it may be equally valid to identify the special market (see 2.12). So, for example, if, at the time of the valuation, a known special market exists such that an intermediary purchaser could acquire the asset and sell on through that special market at a profit, that may have an appreciatory effect on the value of the asset.

If a subsequent sale shows there is a material difference between the share value ascertained and a subsequent actual price obtained, the valuer would do well to check his valuation to see whether revisions are necessary or differences can be accounted for, or whether, as a practical matter, it would be more appropriate to accept Shares Valuation Division's valuation.

In the case of a valuation already agreed with Shares Valuation Division a subsequent sale (which means where all approaches and negotiations commence after the valuation date) should have no influence. If the valuation is still being negotiated, a subsequent sale should have no more influence than a prior sale.

## 2.16 Discount for lack of marketability

The discount for lack of marketability comes into play

when the valuation is based on a comparison with Stock Exchange quoted company shares. The argument is that the purchaser's required yield will be greater for the non-quoted company because its shares are not so easily marketable as quoted company shares and because private company shares are usually subject to restrictions on transfer in the Articles of Association (see 2.13) — a problem accentuated for the minority shareholder.

To give effect to this increased yield factor in a valuation it would be normal to discount the value by an appropriate rate. For minority interests, established practice appears to put this rate somewhere between 25% and 50% with most cases falling between 30% and 40%, the mean rate being slightly greater than 35%. For shareholdings between 50% and 75% discounts should range between 25% and 15%; for 75% to 90% holdings a range of 15% to 7.5% is appropriate, with a 5% to 10% range applicable to 90% + holdings.

The foregoing applies to trading companies. For investment companies some limited assistance may be had from *Battle* v *IRC*, where the Inland Revenue argued that the discount from the value of a 49% interest in an investment company should be 12.5%. First, the "investment" company was really a tax avoidance vehicle and secondly, the 12.5% was a composite discount including: the disadvantage of holding investments through the medium of a company as against holding them personally; the onerous restrictions on transfer of the shares under the company's Articles; and the fact that a minority interest meant the investor could not actually take out of the company the proceeds from the realisation of its investments.

All these facts considered, perhaps 12.5% discount for a minority shareholding is not ungenerous. The Capital Taxes Office actually argued a higher discount, of 15%. Since this discount was agreed by the courts for a company without liabilities and having its assets in a readily realisable form, the discount for a less "cash-like" company or a trading company must be rather more substantial.

The greater the financial risk to the capital, and the greater the marketing problem compared with the quoted company, the higher the discount for non-marketability. Conversely, the more attractive the share the lower the discount that can be justified; shares in a well stocked and well-managed property investment company may be relatively easy to sell provided there is no adverse economic climate at the time.

# Chapter 3

# Shares

## 3.1 Shares and shareholdings

Any share valuation of course starts with the shares themselves. It is necessary to understand precisely what a "share" is and what it means to the person who possesses it. In the Companies Act 1985 s.744, "share" is defined as a "share in the share capital of a company, and includes stock (except where a distinction between shares and stock is express or implied)." Perhaps the most important gloss on this definition can be found in the case of *Borland's Trustees* v *Steel Bros & Co Ltd* in which Farwell J said:

> "A share is the interest of the shareholder in the company measured by a sum of money, for the purpose of liability in the first place, and of interest in the second, but also consisting of a series of mutual covenants entered into by all the shareholders inter se in accordance with [what is now Companies Act 1985 s.14]. The contract contained in the Articles of Association is one of the original incidents of the share."

He went on to say that "A share is not a sum of money but is an interest measured by a sum of money and made up of various rights contained in the contract, including the right to a sum of money of a more or less amount."

The *Borland* case was considered in the estate duty case of *A-G* v *Jameson*, in which Kenny J said:

> "No shareholder has a right to any specific portion of the company's property and save by, and to the extent

of, his voting power at a general meeting of the company, cannot curtail the free and proper disposition of it. He is entitled to a share of the company's capital and profits . . . If the company disposes of its assets, or if the latter be realised in a liquidation, he has a right to a proportion of the amount received after the discharge of the company's debts and liabilities. In applying these rights — that is, in becoming a member of the company — he is deemed to have simultaneously entered into a contract under seal to conform to the regulations contained in the Articles of Association [Companies Act 1985 ss.14 and 22]. Whatever obligations are contained in these Articles . . . they are inseparable incidents attached to his rights and the idea of a share cannot . . . be complete without their inclusion."

In the estate duty case of *IRC* v *Crossman*, Lord Russell of Killowen said of a share:

"it is the interest of a person in the company, that interest being composed of rights and obligations which are defined by the Companies Act and by the Memorandum and Articles of Association of the company."

Thus, these cases show that a share comprises a bundle of rights, but that the shareholder has no right to any specific part of the underlying assets of the company *per se*.

In the case of *Short* v *Treasury Commissioners*, concerning the nationalisation of Short Brothers, Evershed LJ said that "Shareholders are not, in the eye of the law, part owners of the undertaking. The undertaking is something different from the totality of the shareholding." This is a major principle, and later on in the case Evershed took the point that the Crown was acquiring all the shares of the company and thereby, of course, had full control, but pointed out that the Crown was acquiring shares from a number of individual shareholders. He said:

"Prima facie, as it seems to us . . . each shareholder is entitled to get, and to get only the value of what he possesses; that is all that he has to sell or transfer. If an individual shareholder . . . owns such a number of shares . . . as gives him effective control . . . it may well

> be that the value to be attributed to that holding . . . is a figure greater than the sum arrived at by multiplying the number of his shares by the market value for the time being of a single share. In such a case, the shareholder . . . has and is able to sell something more than a mere parcel of shares, each having the rights as to dividend and otherwise conferred upon it by the company's regulations."

On the facts as found in the case, the vendor minority shareholder could have got 29/3d for each of his ordinary shares from a willing buyer; for nationalisation compensation however he claimed a larger sum to reflect the fact that there was added or control value which was also being acquired by the Crown. Evershed summed up his view by saying that he could see no reason in principle why the claimant should receive more than the value of what he had to sell. However, Evershed had not considered the problem of oppression of minority interests where the principle is complicated by minority shareholders being put in an untenable position, especially in cases of "quasi-partnerships"; see 2.14.

## 3.2 Memorandum and Articles of Association

It will be appreciated from the foregoing that, early in the valuation, the valuer should inspect the company's own Memorandum and Articles of Association; and, so far as relevant Tables A, D or E (the latter relating to special classes of company limited by guarantee or unlimited) as published by the Secretary of State (see Companies Act 1985 ss.7-21).

Companies Act 1985 s.14 states:

> "Subject to the provisions of this Act, the Memorandum and Articles, when registered, bind the company and its members to the same extent as if they respectively had been signed and sealed by each member, and contained covenants on the part of each member to observe all the provisions of the Memorandum and of the Articles."

These documents as originated and properly amended set forth the full rights, entitlements, constraints and limitations relating to the shares of the company and they can be investigated at the company's registered office or through a search at Companies House. This latter course of action is rather unsatisfactory but should be taken if there is any possibility that the statutory affairs of the company are incomplete or not up to date. This matter and the problems relating to information generally are discussed at 2.6.

Apart from the Memorandum and Articles of Association there is always the possibility that a shareholders' agreement exists (see 3.4 below), and, unfortunately, there are also circumstances for which the Memorandum and Articles and shareholders' agreement do not cater. An example is the case of an exact balance of power over the control of the company: eg two shareholders each having 50% of the voting power and neither having a casting vote.

## 3.3 Dead-lock ownership/control

The problem of balance of power was examined in the case of *B W Noble Ltd* v *IRC*, in which case a shareholder held 50% of the ordinary shares. In normal circumstances of course that would not bestow control upon that particular shareholder. However, in this case the shareholder was also Chairman of the company. Rowlatt J said that a controlling interest is with the shareholder whose holding in the company is such that he is more powerful than all the other shareholders put together in general meeting. In this case, the shares held by the Chairman were reinforced by the position that he occupied as Chairman:

> "A position that he occupies not merely by the votes of the other shareholders or of his directors elected by the shareholders, but by contract and so reinforced inasmuch as he has casting vote, he does control the general meetings, there is no question about that, and inasmuch as he does possess at least half of the shares, he can prevent any modifications taking place in the constitution of the company which would undermine his position as Chairman."

In situations such as these, thought should be given to precisely what is being valued and placed in the hypothetical market to be sold — and acquired. In a situation as in *Noble* above, the chairman has control whilst he has the two elements — the shares and the contract as chairman which gives him the casting vote. If he could in law sell both the shares, and the chairman's contract of employment with the casting vote, as one package, he would have the ability to sell a controlling interest; but if he cannot sell this package, at the best, he is selling a dead-locked holding. Indeed it may even be a minority interest if the chairman's casting vote remains with or is transferred to another.

If the casting vote or the chairmanship rotates between board members at general meeting, it is unlikely that on a valuation for capital transfer tax/inheritance tax and capital gains tax purposes the dead-locked shareholding could be valued as a controlling interest because the casting vote is a mere transient power and not unfettered. Where there are no specific powers in the Articles of Association to remove a chairman who has a permanent office and casting vote the *Noble* principle will apply and the problem that could arise for CTT/IHT purposes is that the holding might be valued as a controlling interest even though it may not be possible to transfer the casting vote, and any actual sale would be of a dead-locked holding only. One could, of course, argue that the open market value of the "controlling interest" would only equate with a "dead-lock" value because in the open market that is all that would be actually sold and purchased — unless the fact is that the casting vote was capable of travelling with the shares, perhaps because of provisions in the Articles of Association.

A tax problem would arise if a permanent casting vote was transferred, perhaps to a connected party, as this could be regarded as a diminution in value of the transferor's estate (Capital Transfer Tax Act 1984 s.3) and unless it could be argued that the disposition was not intended to confer a gratuitous benefit on the recipient (Capital Transfer Tax Act 1984 s.10) a CTT/IHT exposure could follow. Also, a capital gains tax problem might ensue on the basis that a permanent casting vote could be regarded as an asset (and particularly the provisions of Finance Act 1985 s.71 could be in point). Certainly, a contract of employment is an asset although not capable of being assigned (see *Benson's Hosiery (Holdings) Ltd* v *O'Brien*).

Now consider the other 50% shareholder. If the controlling chairman has no intention of selling his shares, the other 50% shareholder has only a large minority shareholding to sell, whose value may be influenced by matters such as the terms of the chairman's contract or the age of the chairman.

The concept of quasi-partnership may be relevant to deadlock situations (see 2.14) but only for purposes of compulsory winding up (see *Re Yenidje Tobacco Co Ltd*). It may also have some relevance to share valuations in divorce cases where husband and wife are shareholders in a quasi-partnership company, with the result that a valuation may be on the basis of a *pro rata* share of the value of the business as a whole rather than on a discounted minority interest basis.

In the case of *IRC* v *J Bibby & Sons Ltd* it was held that control must be ascertained by reference to the company's constitution and that it is irrelevant that a shareholder who has apparent control may himself be amenable to some external control. In the case of *Barclays Bank* v *IRC* it was found that where a shareholder held 1,100 ordinary shares in his own right and 3,650 shares as trustee, because *under the constitution of the company* he was entitled to vote in respect of both of the holdings and together they constituted more than 50% of the shares in issue, the shareholder had control of the company. Viscount Simmons in that case said that he could see no difference between the natural meaning of the two phrases "having a controlling interest in the company" and "having control of the company", although he felt it might be desirable in the latter case to give an extended meaning to those words. Although under Finance Act 1940 s.55 (estate duty provisions) fiduciary holdings were not to be aggregated with other shareholdings by the same person for estate duty valuation purposes, it was held that this exclusion was not to apply where the fiduciary holding was held by a trustee who was also the settlor. In other words, it was not possible to fragment value by settling shares on oneself to hold some in a fiduciary capacity and some in a personal capacity.

## 3.4 Shareholders' agreements

Usually, such an agreement concerns the division between the parties of profits or assets on a liquidation, or pre-emption rights and restrictions on transfer. The division of profits or assets may be in proportions that differ from the respective shareholdings of those parties and may be calculated by reference to remuneration or management fees drawn by one or other of the parties. In some cases the agreement may provide for a specific profit division for a determinable period and thereafter a different division may apply; in other cases the "rights" attaching to different classes of share ("A" ordinary and "B" ordinary) may be specified or qualified.

The agreement might constitute an agreement to purchase shares or an option to buy or sell; on the other hand, it may in effect be no more than a service contract or management contract. In some cases, it may be a document that evidences the holding of shares in trust for another party: this may be as bare trustee or the shares may be held on trust for sale. The possibilities are just short of endless.

The first step is to ascertain whether the agreement constitutes an enforceable contract, whether standing alone or in conjunction with other document(s), including the company's Memorandum and Articles of Association.

If it does not, it is unlikely to have any serious effect on the value of the shares in point, but nevertheless it may be clear evidence of some management style, third-party influence over the conduct of the business (but note the *IRC* v *J Bibby & Sons Ltd* case at 3.3 above), or other relevant matter.

If it does constitute an enforceable contract it is necessary to determine whether it is in effect an "appendix" to the Memorandum and Articles of Association, in which case it may have an effect on the value of the shares in point and must be read in conjunction with the Memorandum and Articles (see 2.13), or whether it constitutes a personal arrangement that has no intrinsic effect on the shares themselves or on their transferability. If there is some effect, does the agreement continue in force after a transfer or after the death of the shareholder, and is the agreement assignable?

If it is discovered that the shares are simply held on trust or that an option to purchase (or sell) is in existence, it may be necessary to reconsider whether the share valuation exercise being carried out is actually relevant. In the case of the shares held on bare trust or trust for sale, the person in whose name the shares are registered will have no beneficial interest in them (but note the case of *Barclays Bank Ltd* v *IRC*, at 3.3 above) and is not entitled to benefit personally from any rights that the shares may have. If the shares are being valued for the person who does have the ultimate beneficial interest then no problem arises, provided the beneficial interest is unequivocal. If that is not the case, the document must be scrutinized to see from when it took effect, and other enquiries made to determine whether an earlier transfer by the registered owner had taken place. This will be particularly important in any tax related valuation.

In the case of an option to buy or sell where an option price is fixed there will be no valuation requirement (subject to tax considerations). But the option price may, of course, be "market value" (see 2.2) or some other basis such as "fair value" (see 2.10).

A shareholders' agreement may not actually be in writing but without any admission by the shareholders of such agreement or practice and evidence of it, it would be rash to make any valuation adjustment.

## 3.5  The subject of the valuation

Shares are valued according to their entitlement to:

- earnings;
- dividends;
- assets;
- a combination of these factors.

A valuation of shares is concerned with determining the extent of such entitlement, each of which is discussed in detail in the following Chapters.

The first step is to identify what entitlement or "right" attaches to the particular shares which are the subject of the valuation. A number of different types of share may be authorised by a company's Articles of Association, and, as has been seen, the Articles contain regulations governing the allotment and issue of the shares that are so authorised. If a new class of share is to be issued by the company and the Articles do not authorise the issue of such shares, it will be necessary to alter the Articles in accordance with company law. This will require a special resolution and will be minuted. Other relevant matters — such as dividend policy — may be minuted and therefore a share valuation should include inspection of the company's Memorandum and Articles and, if possible, minute book (see 2.6).

In a full valuation of shares it will always be necessary to identify the different classes of share that a company has in issue, their respective entitlements, the number of shares in issue and who owns them beneficially, whether "family" or third parties. Certainly, for tax valuation purposes, if not for other commercial purposes, the relationship between shareholders may be of crucial importance (see, eg, 8.2).

Some of the classes and types of share that may be issued by a company are:

*Ordinary shares:*
- A, B or C, etc, ordinary shares
- preferred ordinary shares
- deferred shares

*Preference shares:*
- fixed preference shares
- participating preference shares
- cumulative preference shares

There may also be:

- employee shares
- phantom shares

and other labelled shares.

### Ordinary shares

The "Ordinary" share is the class of share most commonly met in practice. Such shares usually carry unfettered voting rights for use at shareholders' meetings, most usually the company's Annual General Meeting. They constitute the risk capital put up by the owners of the company and typically are entitled to all of the dividends declared by the directors out of the profits (or accumulated profits) of the company. Should the company be dissolved then its net assets would be distributed to the ordinary shareholders in proportion to their shareholdings. Such distribution may be in cash and/or *"in specie"* (eg where a shareholder takes a car or a property or some other asset in full or partial satisfaction of his rights to a liquidation distribution).

However, this assumes that there are no shares other than ordinary shares. If there are, the terms of the other shares may affect the rights of the ordinary shareholder to receive dividends or liquidation distributions.

For example, where there are "A" ordinary shares and "B" ordinary shares, both carrying voting rights, the "A" ordinary shares may carry equal rights to dividends with the "B" shares, but the "B" shares may carry no rights to a liquidation distribution. It is possible that in such a case there will be a shareholders' agreement which requires the "A" shareholders to vote for a good proportion of the annual profits to be paid out as dividends because the "B" shareholders' only right is to income, not to net assets and reserves, and if they missed a year's profits because no dividend was declared they might lose the right to that income for ever. Alternatively the "B" shares may be entitled to receive a proportion of the accumulated profits on a distribution.

The rights attaching to any class of share can be simple or

complex and it is important to identify them. In the above case, clearly the value of the "A" shares would be greater than the "B" shares, because in addition to the income entitlement that the "A" shareholders share with the "B" shareholders, the "A" shareholders have the sole right to receive any assets of the company on a liquidation.

Yet another possibility frequently met in practice is that some ordinary shares have no voting rights but otherwise rank *pari passu* with the other ordinary shares, so they would be equally entitled to dividends and a liquidation distribution but would have no ability through voting power to influence the activities of the company, including the dividend policy and special resolution required to put the company into liquidation. Similarly, one might find "C" ordinary shares, or "D" ordinary shares and so on. In valuing such shares it will be necessary to have regard to any shareholders' agreement — including possibly an unwritten agreement where it appears that a definable practice has been followed; this may be construed as an established dividend policy, and dividend policies do play an important part when valuing shares on a dividend basis (see Chapter 4).

*Preferred ordinary shares*

These are shares with special rights attaching to them which differentiate them from the other shares in issue. It may be that such shares are entitled to the company's dividends up to some specified limit before the ordinary shareholders can take their dividends, or they may be entitled to some share in the assets on a liquidation. It does not necessarily mean that they are more valuable than the ordinary shares in issue and it is not unusual to find that the right is limited to a fixed rate of dividend, taken before the ordinary dividend, but without the unlimited potential of the ordinary shares — see *Fixed Preference Shares* below. In valuing preferred shares, a proper measure of value must be ascribed to each element of preferential treatment which should be identifiable from the Articles of Association or in a document appended to or forming part of the minutes of the share-holders' or directors' meetings.

*Deferred shares*

There are two principal types of share having deferred rights:

(1) it may be that the holder of such shares will have to wait a specified number of years, perhaps as many as 25, before the shares become entitled to participate at all (whether in dividend or assets), and of course it is almost impossible to determine the state of a company so far into the future. The degree of uncertainty is very great, and what one is valuing in shares that will one day rank *pari passu* with all the then existing ordinary shares, is today's value of that future promise.

One method of valuation is to take the present day value of the ordinary shares, dilute that value by bringing in the number of deferred shares to rank *pari passu* and then discount that diluted value by the appropriate rate over the period of deferral. The appropriate rate may be the real current rate of inflation.

So, if 10,000 shares are in issue, valued at £12 each, and there are 5,000 deferred shares which will rank *pari passu* in 20 years, the diluted value is:

$$\frac{10,000}{10,000 + 5,000} \quad \text{x £12} = \text{£8}$$

Discounted at, say, 7% over 20 years, this becomes *£1.87* (subject to a "risk" discount).

(2) Alternatively, it may be that the shares are labelled deferred because they carry rights to dividends only after the preferred and the ordinary shareholders have received their dividends by reference to some specified limit, after which the deferred shares may have equal rights with the ordinary shares to the residual distributable profits.

An issue of deferred shares often forms part of an estate planning exercise whereby the future worth of a company (if anything) can be passed to future generations at a low, risk, value. Normally, under the articles, no dividends would be payable on such deferred shares and they would carry no voting rights until a specified future date. Usually the Articles would exclude the existing shareholders from diluting the value of the deferred shares by creating more shares.

## Fixed preference shares

Such shares are usually entitled to a fixed "coupon", or rate of dividend which will be payable out of distributable profits before the ordinary shareholders can take the balance. The dividend rate may be 4.5%, 6% or whatever is commercial in relation to the funds injected into the company, the need for the funds, the timing and so on. On the liquidation of the company, preference shareholders will usually be entitled to receive back their original capital before the ordinary shareholders can participate in the surplus net assets. It is unlikely that such preference shareholders will have voting rights, although this is not unknown. What can be found is that preference shareholders have votes concerning the declaration of dividends (to ensure they get some annual return, although unless the company's Articles of Association provide otherwise it is established company law that the dividend on preference shares is cumulative). Such shares would not usually carry rights to vote on any other matter.

If the shares are "redeemable' the company can repay the capital at some future time without having to go into liquidation. Depending on the precise terms of the share issue, there may be a specified date on which, or a specified period during which, the redemption can take place — or there may be no such date. The redemption price may be stated or it may be open. Usually the redemption will be at par (ie the value when issued), but it may be at a premium or a discount — the first to reflect a low rate of interest, the latter to reflect a high rate. The Articles of Association may allow preference shares to participate in liquidation surpluses. Usually on a liquidation, repayment of preference shares takes priority over the repayment of ordinary shares but not over mortgages or debentures.

The normal valuation basis of such shares is the dividend yield (subject, as always, to ascertaining the full rights attaching to the shares). It is usual to identify the yield from quoted preference shares of a similar character. This is discussed in more detail at 3.6.

*Participating preference shares*

Subject to the precise rights, which will be found in the company's Articles of Association, these preference shares would normally be entitled to participate in distributions relating to the ordinary share capital — ie, after fixed and non-participating preference shareholders etc, have been paid out. There may be no right to vote attached to these shares, but if there are voting rights the shares would be valued on the same basis as ordinary shares.

*Cumulative preference shares*

Under the rights attaching to these shares, where in any year a company has been unable to pay a dividend on its preference shares, because of lack of profits, the dividend that would have been paid is effectively reserved until the company has the funds to enable it to distribute the backlog and to continue the payment of dividends on the preference shares. This accumulated reserve must be paid to the preference shareholders before the ordinary shareholders are entitled to receive the dividend. Preference shares are usually cumulative automatically unless specific provision otherwise is made, either in the terms of the issue or under the Articles.

*Employee shares*

Under various incentive schemes, whether devised by individual companies or which follow the rules laid down in share scheme tax legislation, a growing number of organisations give their employees shares or options to acquire shares in the company. These may be non-voting shares and may be required to be surrendered to other employees or shareholders if the holder leaves employment. In some cases there will be restrictions on disposal and the shares may be held by trustees on behalf of the individual employees. In certain arrangements involving employee trusts, the "dividends" paid to the employee may be treated not as investment income but as emoluments from the employment (see Chapter 8).

If the employee shares are special shares then clearly the terms on which they have been — or are to be — issued must be considered. If there are any options in existence in the hands of employees the terms on which the options were given must be examined; the timing of the exercise of the option, the price and from whom the shares are to come (company or shareholder) are all relevant (See Chapter 8). The effect of such shares on the other shares of the company will usually be minimal but clearly this depends upon the number of shares in issue and the number of "new" shares that may be issued on the exercise of the option(s).

If the shares are ordinary shares or otherwise rank *pari passu*, the normal criteria apply for valuation, subject to the subtle differences that exist between valuations for income tax and for capital gains or capital transfer tax/inheritance tax.

## Phantom shares

The phantom share concept developed to reward employees for their special contribution to the growth in asset value or earnings of the employing company by giving them a direct interest in profits or capital growth without involving them in real terms in the equity of the company.

In tax terms this is a most uncertain area and the tax consequences — for both individual and company — will depend upon the circumstances. An income tax charge normally accrues in respect of any receipts by the individual arising from "ownership" of or entitlement to the phantom stock, but, given the right circumstances the "share" might be regarded as a "chose in action" with capital gains tax as well as income tax consequences.

Although the existence of such shares may not affect the rights attaching to equity share capital it may very well have an effect on the company's own obligations and on net distributable profits and assets available for distribution on a liquidation, and thereby could affect the value of the equity shares.

Phantom stock would not usually be regarded as part of the company's capital structure although, by virtue of the phantom stock, there may be arrangements in force which restrict the directors' (or shareholders') actions in some areas, such as declaring dividends, voluntary liquidation of the company or disposal of shares.

## Convertible shares

Where loan stock or shares carry rights of conversion to other classes of share, in valuing the stock, apart from the basic value of the stock itself, the rights of conversion should also be taken into account if there is a measure of value.

An appropriate approach to the valuation is to calculate the value of the shares as if the conversion took place at the date of valuation, and then apply the discount factor which would have to be brought into effect as explained for deferred shares (taking into account any cost of conversion in terms of monetary contribution, or the loss (or gain) of other rights).

## Loan capital — debentures

Debentures carry their own terms and it should normally be possible to value a debenture by looking at the terms under which it is issued. It is unlikely that terms would be found in the Articles of Association but they may be found in the directors or shareholders' minutes or under a deed. If unsecured the loan may have to be valued for the purposes of the loan creditor on a hope-value basis that may well take into account the company's previous dealings with loans and debentures, the personal standing of the individuals involved, even perhaps the relationship between the lender and borrower. It may also be relevant to look for side agreements which may be actionable in law even if not evident on a shallow inspection of the affairs of a company. The hope-value approach would not be appropriate however if a commercial rate of interest is being paid.

Most debentures are entitled to a fixed or determinable rate of interest (rather than a dividend) paid under deduction of income tax. The redemption date (ie the date on which the loan is repayable) may also have some bearing on the matter, as may the terms for repayment, for example the repayment may carry a premium.

Debenture stock and loan stock consist of a number of negotiable units which are marketable in their own right. A large commitment to such stock by a company must be considered very carefully indeed for it is possible for a large stockholding to carry effective control of the company, depending upon the terms of the issue and of the other shareholdings. For example, a minority ordinary shareholding when combined with high coupon loan stock might give effective control over the affairs of the company, including its dividend policy.

## 3.6 Valuing fixed interest securities

To value any fixed-interest stock, a number of factors need to be determined. First, the actual or probable date of redemption of the stock must be known. This may be a fixed date or floating. The terms of the redemption — at par, at a premium or at a discount — must also be ascertained.

Naturally, the coupon (ie the nominal rate of interest payable on the debenture) must be taken into account, as must the timing of interest payments — usually half yearly on gilt edged securities. The coupon itself usually remains constant through to redemption.

If there is no ascertainable redemption date, what is to be valued is the infinite stream of interest payments. Otherwise, the value to be determined is the current market value of the right to receive the fixed interest payments through to redemption plus the redemption monies in due course. Here, the current market value is computed by discounting all future payments to a present day value. This is done by identifying a required rate of return (otherwise known as the redemption yield) and discounting by that rate. This can be readily achieved by adopting mathematical formulae as follows:

*Example:*

To value, at 1 January 1986, 1000 x £1 (6%) debentures redeemable on 31 July 1993 at a premium of 15%. Interest is payable half-yearly. The required redemption yield at 1 January 1986 is, say, 16% p.a., or 8% per half year. There are 7.5 years to redemption which comprises 15 half yearly periods.

The formula to use is:

$$\text{Value} = \frac{r}{y} + \frac{R - \frac{r}{y}}{(1+y)^t}$$

where:

r is the nominal rate of interest expressed as a
   decimal (per half year is 3%) =     0.03
y is the required redemption yield expressed as a
   decimal (per half year is 8%) =     0.08
R is the redemption value of the security where
   par is 1 (at a 15% premium) =     1.15
t is the number of years (or half years) to
   redemption =     15

$$\text{So: } \frac{.03}{.08} + \frac{1.15 - \frac{.03}{.08}}{(1+.08)^{15}}$$

$$= 0.375 + \frac{0.775}{3.172}$$

$$= 0.619 \text{ or (say) } 62\%.$$

Therefore each £1 of stock is worth *62p*.

The required (gross) redemption yield can be identified from lists of yields for quoted corporation stock prepared by firms of stockbrokers. Alternatively, average gross redemption yields can be taken from the Financial Times Actuaries Equity Indices which give yields for low, medium and high coupons for each of short-, medium- and long-dated gilts as well as irredeemables, and give average yields for short-, medium- and long-dated debentures and loans.

Because of the problems associated with quoted share comparisons (see 4.7 and 5.4), it is perfectly in order to consider increasing the quoted yield for private company purposes. On the assumption that the private company is secure and there is no fundamental problem in this area, the required yield for private company fixed-interest stock could be taken at around 20% greater than the average yield for debentures or perhaps 25% greater than the average yield for gilts. If a comparable quoted corporation debenture can be found an uplift of around 10% to 15% may be appropriate — it is primarily a question of security. Unlike ordinary and other shares, debentures do not usually carry restrictions on the right to transfer to new ownership, but they are less readily marketable than their quoted cousins. Also, it has to be said that the financial controls on quoted company gearing are likely to be more stringent than for the private company, and while it might not be too difficult for a public company to meets its continuing debt obligations — and particularly the full redemption cost — by the issue of new stock, this may not be the same for the private company. Therefore the debt/equity gearing should be checked. The interest "cover" by income and assets, ie the amount of the interest obligation covered by the company's profits and/or net assets, should be satisfactory. The rights attaching to the loan stock on a liquidation or on a failure to meet interest payments should also be investigated. Any unsatisfactory elements would naturally affect the required yield.

### 3.7 Capitalisation

The specific rights attaching to shares issued by a company will be specified in the company's Articles of Association. Those rights may not be altered without a special resolution being passed either at the annual shareholders' meeting or by an extraordinary shareholders' meeting. Where rights are altered or where a new class of share is to be issued the company's Articles of Association may have to be altered, and this, too, requires a special resolution. It may be that under the Articles, the directors do have power to issue new shares and to determine the rights attaching to those shares.

A company may revise its capital structure from time to time by making bonus or scrip issues of shares or by offering new shares for subscription. This is done to help keep the balance between capital employed, current earnings and dividends on an even commercial keel. For example, in its early years of trading a company may have an issued share capital of 10,000 £1 ordinary shares and assets of £10,000, earning £5,000 per year; from these earnings a dividend payment of (say) 10% of £10,000 (£1,000) could be made.

Some years later, the company's assets may have grown to £200,000 and its earnings to £50,000. It might be that its annual dividends now are £10,000, i.e. 100% of the issued share capital. A bonus of 9:1 would improve the ratios, making the issued share capital (after the bonus) £100,000 and the dividend yield would be 10% rather than 100%. The value of the shares as a whole remains the same, although each share is a smaller proportionate amount of the entire share capital. This may also make it easier to dispose of small parcels of shares either by gift or sale.

Often, such a bonus issue would be followed by a declaration that future dividend rates are to increase (from 10% say, to 12%). Such announcements may be very relevant in a share valuation exercise. In fact any statement as to future dividend policy is obviously of some interest.

A *rights issue* is made when a company wishes to attract

more capital, maybe as working capital or for some specific expansion purpose. In such cases, existing shareholders are circularised with details of the issue and are usually offered favourable terms if they take up some of the additional shares before a specified date.

At the end of the exercise — when the share capital becomes "ex rights", the par value of the new share capital will equal the par value of the old shares plus the new money attracted by the rights issue. If new shares were issued "at a premium" this means that the shares have been subscribed for at a price higher than the par value. In this case the company's balance sheet will include a "share premium" reserve as part of the shareholders' capital. The premium will belong to the company and thereby for the benefit of all the shareholders, not just those who paid the premium. However, there are some capitalisation methods that leave the value of the original share capital largely unaffected. This is achieved where a new class of share or security is issued. So, for example, if there are 10,000 x £1 shares in issue in a company and it wished to attract new capital of, say, £40,000, typically there would first be a bonus issue of ordinary shares — let us say 10 for 1 so the shares become 100,000 x 10p shares, but the total current market value of those 10p shares would be the same as the total value of the £1 shares. Then the company would issue £40,000 x £1 participating preference shares.

## 3.8 Shareholdings

It will be appreciated that one of the first steps is to ascertain the types of share in issue, and the rights attaching to those shares whether specified in the company's Articles of Association, an agreement or other arrangements. It is equally important to establish that all issues have been made properly under the correct powers. Then it is necessary to identify the history of issues, dividends and redemption, and to ascertain what policy decisions have been taken concerning future redemption, issues or dividends.

This forms the basic information necessary to identify what is to be valued, and it also provides the full background to the "environment" within which the subject of the valuation lies.

There are four standard bases for valuing company shares:

- the dividend basis (Chapter 4);
- the earnings basis (Chapter 5);
- the asset basis (Chapter 6);
- the hybrid basis (Chapter 7).

Whichever basis should be adopted in any particular case depends upon the circumstances. The first indication of the appropriate basis will be found from the size of the shareholding that is being valued, as explained below.

Having identified the "rights" attaching to the shares in issue, it is necessary to ascertain the total value attributable to each class of share.

The next step is to consider that value in relation to the total number of shares held by any one shareholder, either directly or perhaps through a trustee or nominee. An important point here is that for tax purposes all the shares held by "connected" persons would have to be added together to form a composite shareholding. For a discussion of connected persons and direct and indirect shareholdings, see 8.2 and 8.3.

In the case of fixed-interest stocks and bonds, debentures and so on, it should be possible to determine their value without great difficulty because the terms on which they were issued would normally contain all the information necessary for determining their value at any time. A problem is encountered, however, in establishing the value of shares carrying voting rights, as the value of such a shareholding will not necessarily be a direct proportionate share of the total value of the company. There are certain levels of shareholding at which the value of the shares in the holding will be influenced considerably by force of numbers. This "critical mass" concept is fundamental to choosing the correct valuation basis, but is not the end of the matter. The circumstances surrounding the valuation may require a hybrid basis of valuation to be adopted (see Chapter 7); a non-going concern will invariably require a net assets valuation on a break-up basis; an asset-rich company may require a straight net-assets basis; and tax rules (especially CTT/IHT) may require a basis different from that which would be expected (eg a disposal of a minority interest out of a controlling interest — see 8.3).

## 90% Shareholdings

By virtue of the Companies Act 1985 s.428, the holder of 90% or more of the shares in a company has not only an unfettered right to sell his shares but he can give the purchaser of the shares compulsory powers to enable him to buy all or any of the remaining issued shares whether or not the other shareholders wish to sell. The holder of 90% or more shares has total control over the direction of the company, its dividend policies and so on.

## 75% Shareholder

The holder of 75% or more of the shares has sufficient power to pass a special resolution to put the company into liquidation or to sell the business as a going concern. Although he cannot engineer the sale of 100% of the shares of the company to a single purchaser, in other respects he has effective control over the company.

*Valuation note:* The lowest valuation that could be placed upon a shareholding of 75% to 100% would be the value of the liquidated assets after meeting all expenses of the liquidation such as redundancy payments, deferred taxation and direct costs of the liquidation. The direct costs of the liquidation may be in the order of 25% to 33% of the value of the liquidated assets. The value of the liquidated assets may be determined under the break-up value principles, see 6.2. But one would only adopt that value if there was a likelihood that the "asset-stripper" principle applies, ie that a purchaser would do better to buy the liquidated assets than the company out of which they come (eg because the company has a history of losses and under-utilisation of assets), or would purchase the company to strip the assets out himself.

In the case of a going concern the usual valuation base for 75%+ shareholdings would be the earnings basis.

### 50%+ Shareholder

The shareholder with more than 50% of the voting shares has the day to day control of the company. This shareholding gives effective control as the shareholder can appoint himself or his nominees as directors in charge of the company's business (albeit, possibly at a cost if the consequences of so doing would be to effect a constructive dismissal of existing directors).

*Valuation note:* Usually, a holding of 50%+ of the shares would be valued on the basis of the earnings of the company, such as by reference to the last three years' available accounts profits but with reference to profit trends, cyclical business, known economic facts and so on, subject to the points made above generally and in relation to 75% shareholdings.

### 50% Shareholder

A 50% shareholder does not have control, but then neither does any other party unless additional factors provide that shareholder with the effective control over the company, such as a casting vote at meetings (see 3.3).

*Valuation note:* If effective control can be shown then the shares would be valued as though the holder owned 50%+ shares, and the valuation would then usually be on an earnings basis, but subject to the points made above. If there is no effective control, however, the value of the shares will probably be based on the dividend yield, and this depends on the dividend policy of the company. All the factors are looked at with an eye to determining whether dividend policies will be maintained or whether the likelihood of future dividends will be strengthened or lessened.

It may also be useful to see whether the shareholder has a contract of employment with the company under which he receives remuneration. If it can be shown that the employment would cease and no-one would take the place of that individual or take the remuneration himself, then it may be reasonable to expect an increased dividend payment. Indeed, it would be perfectly reasonable to proceed in valuing the shareholding on the basis of the payment of notional dividends where the policy is not to take dividends but to accrue profits or pay them all in remuneration and benefits to shareholders. This approach is fraught with difficulties and there must be evidence that the transmutation of remuneration into dividend income is a reasonable possibility. One would have to view the decisions of the board of directors as being rational and assume that dividends would be paid according to the company's trading results and business requirements. A starting point for estimating a notional dividend (and it is no more than a starting point) would be to take one-sixth of the available profit after corporation tax and discount it on the grounds that the dividend is only notional. The rate of discount would reflect the degree of certainty of real dividends reaching the new shareholders. For a fuller discussion, see 4.4, 4.6.

*25%+ Shareholder*

A shareholder having 25% or more of the shares in the company can block a special resolution for the liquidation or disposal of the company. A shareholding of anything from 33% upwards may be in the area of effective control, depending upon the full circumstances. The Shares Valuation Division regard any 25%+ shareholding as an "influential minority shareholding" which means that they would expect the value of each share to be greater than a share in a "small minority shareholding" — ie under 25%. However, it should also be realised that a shareholding as high as 49% may be totally without influence if 51% is owned by a single party.

*Under 25% Shareholders*

This shareholding (small minority shareholding) would also be valued on a dividend yield basis. In normal investment terms no-one would acquire such a shareholding unless:

(a) a high yield is available to compensate for the vulnerability of the shareholding to special resolutions against which it would not be effective; or

(b) it was to be added to other shares in the company to create a majority shareholding and thereby give control (and see 2.11).

As a further consideration, where all the shareholders are minority shareholders it may not be possible to discount the value of the shares to the same extent as when a controlling shareholder does exist. Their marketability would be greater, all other things being equal.

*10% or less shareholders*

Such holdings are subject to compulsory acquisition under the Companies Act 1985 s.428 and the dividend yield required from such a shareholding would be greater than that for the larger shareholding which protects the shareholder's position.

# Chapter 4

# The dividend basis

## 4.1 Shareholding influence

The dividend basis of valuation is adopted for a shareholding in a company that is not in danger of being liquidated, where the benefit of holding the shares is manifested principally in the right to receive dividends that flow or may flow from the shareholding.

It is usually found that small minority shareholdings (ie under 25%) have very little prospect of income returns except through the operation of dividend policies of others (ie those having control of the company or the directors), and therefore any value will only be found in the established dividend policies of the company or, in some cases, in "deemed" dividend flows (see below).

For shareholdings between 25% and 50% (influential minority shareholdings), there may be an argument for the earnings basis as opposed to the dividend basis, but only if it could be shown that through some other identifiable power or circumstance the shareholding exerts influence over the way the profits of the company are applied, or over the realisation of assets. See Chapter 7.

For certain tax purposes, "control" can exist if a shareholding exceeds 30% (see Business Expansion Scheme, Finance Act 1981 s.56(8)). Although the context in which that is applicable is very special and ties in with other tax rules, it does illustrate the belief, however tenuous, that a 30%+ shareholding can exert influence, and this would especially be the case where all the other shareholdings are small in comparison. A shareholding of 25% gives the holder power to block a special resolution — see 3.7. A shareholding above 25% would usually give the shareholder the expectation of a seat on the board of directors. This opportunity to exert influence must count for something, although the power to block a special resolution can be regarded more as a power to maintain the *status quo* than a power to influence company policies. The Shares Valuation Division regards holdings between 25% and 50% as "influential minority shareholdings" and in these cases they would normally expect a valuation to be biased towards the price/earnings ratio (see Chapter 5). Whether the assets basis is appropriate will depend largely upon the size of the shareholding and the likelihood of an early liquidation, and this is discussed below in more detail.

The influence of a shareholding *per se* should not be confused with the personal influence exerted by an individual through common sense or personal persuasive attributes; neither can be it a factor for tax valuation purposes.

## 4.2 Possible liquidation

Assuming that the shareholding to be valued does not exert any particular influence over the management or policy-making machinery of the company, the minority shareholder will find that the only benefit arising from holding the shares will be the flow of dividends, if any, plus (usually) the right to receive a liquidation distribution should the company be wound up. There is also the ability to re-sell the shares (subject to restrictions on transfer where relevant), but this "ability" may not, and probably will not, have the immediacy of quoted shares. One might even speculate that the investment is tied up for a number of years and, subject to the facts, equate the holding to fixed interest long-dated stock (see 3.6).

The right to receive a liquidation distribution derives its value from the likelihood that the net asset value of the company will be realised in the *foreseeable* future through a liquidation, or through a reorganisation or acquisition of the company's shares.

If liquidation (whether voluntary or otherwise), is a strong possibility; or a takeover is likely; and/or if the character of the asset-backing is substantial (eg land, buildings, intellectual property or substantial reserves), then it may be necessary to consider an asset basis valuation in addition to the dividend basis valuation, or as an alternative to it. This would largely depend upon how soon such a realisation of value might be expected or how "solid" the asset-backing. In the case of a court order for the compulsory winding up of the company under Companies Act 1985 s.461, a *pro rata* valuation basis may apply even though the shareholding is a minority share-holding (see also 2.14).

Dividends emanating from a company with solid asset-backing are assumed more likely to be maintained or to grow than dividends depending upon, for example, a seasonal or a "fashionable" trade. On the other hand, it may be argued that in the immediate or foreseeable future the dividends expected to be earned from a fashionable trade would easily outstrip any dividends backed by traditional assets such as property. Even property values have been known to suffer when least expected. This is where the art of valuing shares shows its ascendancy.

Where a liquidation of a company is expected, the dividend basis cannot be applicable and the only benefit to be had from the shareholding would be the eventual pay-out from the disposal of the company's assets. For this purpose, the likely date of liquidation should be ascertained and the projected asset value given a present day value by discounting over the period of time by the required rate of return (see below). But, of course, the circumstances must be investigated fully before any final decision is made as to which basis is applicable.

If losses are being made but no liquidation is foreseen and no dividends are being paid, the first question to be resolved is "will the company make profits in the future?" If the answer is that profits will be made, it should be possible to quantify the expected profits, dividends and earnings yield, and having done so, to determine a share value on the basis of expecting those dividends — see 4.4 below, where this matter and the question of a discount for uncertainty are discussed.

## 4.3 Expectation of future dividends

If the company is not about to be liquidated, and the asset-backing comprises only fixed assets of no special value, trade debtors and some cash, the shareholder's only expectation from holding the shares is to receive dividends such as he has done in the past. It is this expectation that is valued under the dividend basis.

The first stage is to look at the past dividends (say in the preceding three to five years) and take note of any actual dividend policy. There are four possibilities:

- the dividends are constant year by year;
- the dividends show a steady growth or reduction;
- the dividends fluctuate;
- no dividends (see 4.4).

*Constant dividend*

Taking the first case, let us assume that a dividend of 50p per share is paid each year. Assume also that the current *required rate of return* (see 4.8) from an investment of similar character and risk is 10%. The value of such a share would be that amount which, if yielding 10% per annum, would give 50p. Arithmetically this is calculated quite simply by grossing up 50p as follows:

$$\frac{50p \times 100\%}{10\%} = \underline{£5}$$

(ie Value £5 at 10% = yield of 50p per share)

Often, a dividend is declared as a rate per share (eg 20% per 25p share = 5p dividend). Note that the 25p is the nominal or par value, not the current market value. The current market value of this share, if we continue to assume a *required rate of return* of 10%, would be that amount which, if yielding 10% per annum, would give 20% of 25p. This is calculated as follows:

$$\frac{20\% \times 25p}{10\%} = \underline{£0.50}$$

(ie Value 50p @ 10% = yield of 5p per share; 25p @ 20% = 5p).

## Dividend growth

Suppose that the dividend has been shown to increase each year by an average of 20% gross (of the previous dividend), and that this growth is expected to continue into the foreseeable future. The last dividend declared was 10p which represented a return of 20% on the nominal value of the share which is 50p. One might assume that a respectable required rate of return from any investment made today on similar risk is 12.5% (without reflecting the in-built growth factor). A naive valuation would be simply to take the current dividend and gross it up by the required return. This would give:

(i)    $\dfrac{10p \times 100\%}{12.5\%} = \underline{£0.80}$

(ie Value 80p at 12.5% = yield of 10p per share)

However, the return from the investment made today will be the next dividend, and that will be 20% up on the last dividend. This means the expected dividend will increase by 2p (10p @ 20%). Thus:

(ii)    $\dfrac{10p + 2p \times 100\%}{12.5\%} = \underline{96p}$

(ie Value 96p at 12.5% = yield of 12p per share)

If we had not increased the value of the share to reflect the expected dividend increase, the actual return received on 80p would have been 12p, or 15% — much greater than the required return of 12.5%.

This calculation takes into account the next following dividend but does not reflect the benefit of the constant growth expected. There should be weighting to take this growth factor into account, except to the extent that the *required rate of return* itself includes any growth expectation, for example, if it is derived from dividend yields based on quoted share prices which themselves reflect dividend growth in their quoted company. The growth factor should only be entertained if it is certain that the dividend growth will continue — again, this will depend upon a thorough-going review of the performance of the company.

Such a review would be undertaken to ensure that a recent high or steady dividend record is not being met solely out of retained earnings (which will eventually dry up), and does not arise out of a ploy to defeat an unwelcome take-over bid, but arises out of sound trading results (going back three to five or more years), and all economic and commercial forecasts for the particular business and the industry in general indicate that the growth will continue. It is quite common for dividend payments to be smoothly progressive so far as dividend growth is concerned but for the underlying profits of the company to be more volatile. This is perfectly in order provided that the company's profit velocity is satisfactory, ie that the overall level of profits is increasing against inflation despite *occasional* set-backs whether manifested in a loss or a weaker growth rate one year.

In the case of constant growth the exercise is to ascertain for each share such a value as will provide the required rate of return allowing for the fact that there is an in-built growth in the dividends that are being received. The difficulty is that where there is such in-built dividend growth it is not possible to give a simple valuation that can be stated in terms of an amount which will earn a fixed x% every year.

A compromise must be made at some stage and in the final analysis the question is "would I buy the shares at that price if I were in the market?"

The simplest formula is as follows:

(iii) $$\frac{\text{The first projected dividend}}{\text{Required rate of return} - \text{Dividend growth rate}} \times 100 = \text{Share value}$$

Suppose the nominal value of each share is £1. The latest dividend to be declared was 20p, and over the last five years the dividends have grown at a compound rate of 4% each year (that is 4% of each previous dividend). This growth is fully expected to continue and the required rate of return in an investment of similar risk but without the promise of an annual 4% income growth in addition to capital growth is 11%.

Applying our formula:

$$\frac{20p + (4\% \times 20p)}{11\% - 4\%} = \frac{20p + 0.8p}{7\%} \times 100 = £2.97$$

But £2.97 at the required rate of return of 11% should yield 32.67p not 20p or 20.8p. A justification for the value is illustrated in the following table. The apparent anomaly arises because the required rate of return is by reference to the *total return over the period of ownership* and not merely on a year-by-year basis. So, the investor who is concerned to receive actually, in cash, 11% of his investment each year may simply not be in the market for a shareholding which is providing constant dividend growth.

## Table

| (1) Annual Required Return | (2) Year | (3) 4% Growth Factor | (4) Annual Return (Dividend) | (5) Annual Variance + − (4) − (1) | (6) Total Variance + − | (7) Acquisition (−) Disposal (+) Price | (8) Profit on Disposal (7) - £2.97 | (9) Surplus (8) - (6) |
|---|---|---|---|---|---|---|---|---|
| pence | | pence | pence | pence | pence | £ | £ | pence |
| | 0 | | 20.00 | | | (−2.97) | | |
| 32.67 | 1 | 0.80 | 20.80 | −11.87 | −11.87 | +3.09 | 0.12 | − |
| 32.67 | 2 | 0.83 | 21.63 | −11.04 | −22.91 | +3.21 | 0.24 | 1 |
| 32.67 | 3 | 0.87 | 22.50 | −10.17 | −33.08 | +3.34 | 0.37 | 4 |
| 32.67 | 4 | 0.90 | 23.40 | −9.27 | −42.35 | +3.48 | 0.51 | 9 |
| 32.67 | 5 | 0.94 | 24.34 | −8.33 | −50.68 | +3.62 | 0.65 | 14 |
| 32.67 | 6 | 0.97 | 25.31 | −7.36 | −58.04 | +3.76 | 0.79 | 21 |
| 32.67 | 7 | 1.01 | 26.32 | −6.35 | −64.39 | +3.91 | 0.94 | 30 |
| 32.67 | 8 | 1.05 | 27.37 | −5.30 | −69.69 | +4.07 | 1.10 | 40 |
| 32.67 | 9 | 1.09 | 28.46 | −4.21 | −73.90 | +4.23 | 1.26 | 52 |
| 32.67 | 10 | 1.14 | 29.60 | −3.07 | −76.97 | +4.40 | 1.43 | 66 |
| 32.67 | 11 | 1.18 | 30.78 | −1.89 | −78.86 | +4.57 | 1.60 | 81 |
| 32.67 | 12 | 1.23 | 32.01 | −0.56 | −79.42 | +4.76 | 1.79 | 1.00 |
| 32.67 | 13 | 1.28 | 33.29 | +0.62 | −78.80 | | | |

This table illustrates the required rate of return over the period of ownership of shares receiving dividends growing at 4% per annum.

Column (7) disposal values are each determined using exactly the same formula as used to calculate the market value acquisition price of £2.97.

Suppose the share is disposed of after the dividend is declared in year 4. At that time the cost of acquiring the share is £2.97 and the investment is short of the required return by 42.35p (the deficit total variance shown in Column (6)). Upon a sale of the share at this time the share value calculated on the same basis as when it was acquired would be:

$$\frac{23.4p + (4\% \times 23.4p)}{11\% - 4\%} = \frac{23.4p + 0.94p}{7\%} \times 100\% = £3.48$$

The sale value exceeds the acquisition value by (£3.48 − £2.97) = 51p.

So, at this stage there appears to be an investment deficit (ie the amount by which the actual dividends paid over the four years falls short of the required rate of return) of 42.35p, say 42p, on the one hand and a profit on sale of 51p. A net profit of 9p has been made which recompenses the investor to some extent for the loss of interest on the investment deficit. The 9p net profit can be said to represent simple interest on the accumulating investment deficits of between 8% and 16% p.a. depending upon when in each year the share was bought and sold.

Applying the same principles in year 10 the surplus of 66p in Column (9) represents a simple interest return of between 5% and 6.5%, again depending upon when in each year the share was bought and sold. After year 12, the variance becomes positive − ie the investment starts to earn the 11% directly from the dividend payments.

The same formula must be applied consistently to future disposals because the shares are being valued on the assumption that there will be a constant future stream of dividends with continual growth. Of course, in the future things may well be different, the required rate of return may, in four years time, be greater or less than it is today (probably dependent upon the rate of inflation) but the chances of that happening must be taken into account in determining what is an acceptable and maintainable dividend growth percentage to take into the calculation. All other things being equal, the method of calculating the crystallised value of the future stream of dividends must be the same.

In the case of a constant reduction in the dividend yield naturally the converse applies.

Finally, one should not lose sight of the fact that it is future maintainable dividends that are required to be ascertained, and past performance is nothing more than one of the tools used in determining the answer.

*Fluctuating yields*

In this case it is largely a question of attempting to discern a minimum level of maintainable dividends and to add to that what (if anything) is reasonably certain of being achieved in the future in terms of increased dividends. If the company is large enough and well enough established, it might be helpful to apply the linear trend analysis formula set out at 5.7. Alternatively, the possibilities set out in the following sections of this Chapter may be of assistance.

## 4.4 No dividend record

A problem often encountered is that although the company is profitable it does not actually pay dividends. In these cases it may be appropriate to calculate a notional dividend. One way to compute notional dividends is to divide maintainable earnings (5.6) by the dividend cover (4.8). Dividend cover is the ratio of earnings yield to dividend yield (see 9.20) but, if this approach is to be meaningful, it is important that an independent, empirical figure for cover is used, and not one itself derived from the yield figures. If this warning is ignored, the result will be earnings and dividend basis valuations that are identical, since the latter will then just be another way of calculating the former.

This notional dividend approach would not normally apply if the liquidation of the company was envisaged because in such a case the asset basis would be more appropriate (see Chapter 6). If there really appears to be no chance of future dividends arising and there cannot be said to be an oppression of minorities (see 2.14) then perhaps a hybrid basis (see Chapter 7) is appropriate. The full facts concerning current dividend policies and the possibility of future dividends must be considered carefully and any positive likelihood of dividends should be reflected in the valuation given, either by construction of a notional dividend or by applying a hybrid valuation.

In deciding what the notional dividend should be, the valuer must actually embark upon determining a dividend policy for the company where the policy to date had been not to declare dividends. It is almost a contradiction, but this perversity will be recognised in the discount for uncertainty that must ultimately be applied to the share value determined under the "notional" dividend basis valuation. The valuer must have regard to everything concerning the business and its standing, and the structure of the company, its management and ownership. Is it working at full extent? Are all its profits (now and in the future) taken up in meeting bank interest or on other borrowings or debentures, preference stock etc? What about cash flow requirements, and capital investment commitments in the past, present and future? What are the levels of wages, salaries and fees — are any such payments being made to current shareholders and would such payments cease if the shareholder ceased to be a shareholder? Is the business improving or not? What retentions are necessary for continuing or future business development? Are current reserves sufficient to meet all these real or contingent liabilities? Are current reserves excessive and will they continue to be so?

And when, at last, a notional dividend policy which recommends a notional dividend has been determined — why have the directors not so recommended? Could there be a reason that has not been considered?

An artificial dividend policy being assumed and a value for the shares being determined, what rate of discount for uncertainty should be applied? Perhaps the discount to be considered is really a discount for certainty that the proposed dividends will *not* be declared. After the painstaking effort of arriving at a perfectly reasonable dividend policy on the evidence of past performance, the valuer may well feel that there is a high degree of certainty that future dividends will *not* be declared. If that is not his opinion there is a presumption that the current directors have not been doing their job properly because they had not come to the same conclusion.

As a matter of practice, Shares Valuation Division may allow a discount of 50% in respect of a 10% shareholding. In theory, discount at a much higher level would be justified in some cases, but one would be mistaken not to expect considerable resistance to this. Of course, Shares Valuation Division might agree the higher discount but then take issue with the pre-discount price, questioning the amount of the dividend or the rate of return adopted to determine the value. Nothing would be agreed in isolation and all the facts may have to be aired before the final discounted value is arrived at.

## 4.5 Irregular dividend record

A company's dividend record may not have shown smooth growth over the years, but may have been irregular and intermittent. In such a case a careful appraisal of the past performance of the company should be undertaken. The dividend policy criteria should be investigated to discover the underlying reasons for the way in which dividends have been declared.

The valuer might find himself undertaking a full review of the company's dividend policy, even constructing a new one on the bases of the known earnings of the company and development of the business. Alternatively, (and much more simply) the past dividends can be extrapolated using the linear trend analysis formula set out at 5.7.

Whatever approach is adopted the valuer must continuously remind himself that it is the future maintainable dividends that need to be determined — a future policy that it would be reasonable to suppose will be followed and future level of earnings out of which those dividends would be paid. One is using past performance to help identify the dividend growth factor to apply to the future.

## 4.6 Notional dividends

When notional maintainable future dividends and a dividend growth factor (whether positive, negative or nil) have been determined the required rate of return should be ascertained and then the formula explained at (iii) on page 75 may be applied.

By maintainable dividends is meant a level of dividends — either greater, the same or less than the last dividend — that with reasonable certainty one would expect to find being paid out in future years.

In looking at maintainable dividends the valuer must satisfy himself that the company can continue its current trading pattern for the foreseeable future without any major change in its management, customers and business environment (the fact that the shareholders may not be the same as in the past should not affect this consideration). If no future dividends can be expected, and if the earnings basis and the assets basis have been discarded, all that remains are worthless shares or shares of nominal value only.

See also 4.4 above.

## 4.7 Long established companies

There are some companies whose performance can be gauged over a very long period indeed — much longer than the normal three to ten year spread — and there may well be cases where there are "cycles" in the trading history that can be illustrated over such a period. There is no reason in theory why such trading cycles should not be reflected in a valuation if it is expected that the cycle will continue. A long established fixed growth rate — whether or not adjusted for inflation — may form the mainstay of a share valuation provided it is expected that the growth will continue at that rate. In the *Salveson* and *Holt* cases, the performance of companies over very long periods indeed were considered in the valuation exercise.

But the smoothest of progressions can be interrupted and it really is impossible to say with certainty that a fixed growth rate will continue uninterrupted into the future.

The long-established company can be considered with less scepticism than other companies, but it would be naive to ignore clouds on the horizon. For example, a major research programme which is not 100% funded cannot be said to be a safe bet for the future prosperity of the company. Indeed if the very survival of the company depended upon such a project, the valuer would be well advised to adopt a more sceptical position.

## 4.8 The required rate of return—the quoted company comparison and the alternative

In calculating a share value under the dividend basis principle, it is necessary to identify a required rate of return for the investment that the purchaser of the share (or the deemed purchaser) would have in mind. This is the real return he expects to get for risking his money. Thus, shares with a nominal value of £1 each may be yielding a dividend of 30p per share. If each of those shares were for sale at £3, the dividend of 30p would represent a dividend yield and a rate of return of 10%: the dividend yield is a function of the share value.

The correct formula for determining the dividend yield is:

$$\frac{\text{Nominal value of share}}{\text{Share value}} \times \frac{\text{Dividend as a percentage}}{\text{of Nominal value}}$$

$$= \text{Dividend yield}$$

substituting the above figures:

$$\frac{100p}{300p} \times 30p = 10\%$$

If that value of the shares is unknown, the calculation becomes:

$$\frac{\genfrac{}{}{0pt}{}{\text{Dividend as a percentage}}{\text{of nominal value}}}{\text{Dividend yield}} \times \text{Nominal value of share}$$

$$= \text{Share value}$$

This leads to the crux of the matter. What if neither the value of the share nor the dividend yield is known? The answer is to determine a dividend yield.

Theoretically, the return that the investor will require is the same return that he would get if he invested his capital elsewhere on similar risk with similar growth prospects and with the same ease (or difficulty) of conversion to cash. If no such alternative investment can be identified it becomes a question of looking at what other investments are available and making appropriate adjustments to the yield to compensate for the intrinsic differences between the minority shareholding on the one hand and the alternative investment on the other.

The valuation exercise should have given the valuer a good idea of the financial risk involved in acquiring the shares and the growth prospects. The convertibility to cash will be governed by the problem of selling the shares again, and the valuer will have a view about this also. But, certainly for minority interests, the information that the valuer has about the company would not be available to the share purchaser; see 2.6.

Valuation experts often differ in their approach to identifying the rate of return from a similar investment. It may be appropriate to see what could be earned from investing the same amount of money in a "similar" quoted public company. However, most experts would hold that, certainly for minority shareholdings, there can be no comparison between listed company investment and private company investment. It is a strong argument, supported by the courts. Except in relation to the very largest and quite unrepresentative private companies, the economic suspension in which the quoted company floats is quite different from the private environment.

If it is not possible to identify an alternative comparable investment that carries a specified yield, there is little option left but to take all the available evidence (including quoted company data) and determine where else the money could have gone and at what rate of return.

It is easy to confuse the required rate of return and the dividend yield required. The two may sometimes be the same, but where someone is selling shares which have definite and proven dividend growth the current required dividend yields may be swamped in years to come by future dividend growth, and if this future dividend growth carries an insignificant risk, to value a share today simply on a current dividend yield requirement may be to undervalue the share. This has been illustrated above (see 4.3). But looking then at the required rate of return on a similar investment (ie the minimum return over the period of ownership that one would expect to earn from the investment year by year), how is it to be determined with regard to a private company that has no other exact counterpart?

*Comparing the quoted company*

As a practical matter, Shares Valuation Division will almost certainly attempt to categorise the unquoted company and apply an "equivalent" quoted company yield if it can. In the case of fixed interest securities, SVD would compare quoted company stocks and gilts (see 3.6). Therefore, if in any particular case one wishes to avoid a direct comparison with quoted company yields, it will be necessary to marshal one's reasons. SVD has much experience, a very considerable amount of information on company performance and very practical negotiating skills. Tenacity and perseverance are required.

Before considering how to determine a quoted company comparison, it is fair to point out the courts' displeasure with the ill-considered quoted company comparison. In dismissing the quoted company comparison, some experts will argue that the potential buyers in the quoted company sector are fundamentally different from those in the market for private company shares and this view would be borne out by Danckwerts J in *Re Holt* when he said:

> "I think the kind of investor who would purchase shares in a private company of this kind, in circumstances which must preclude him disposing of his shares freely whenever he should wish (because he will, when registered as a shareholder, be subject to the provisions of the articles restricting transfer) would be different from any common kind of purchaser of shares on the Stock Exchange, and would be rather the

exceptional kind of investor, who had some special reason for putting his money into shares of this kind . . ."

That case concerned a minority shareholding of some 6%. The passage was quoted and supported by Lord Pearson in the *Re Lynall* decision.

In *Re Lynall*, Plowman J in the High Court criticised the quoted company comparison, giving some examples of why the method is unsatisfactory: dividend policies are entirely different; regulations concerning the transfer of shares are entirely different; and, perhaps the most pointed comment of all: "Moreover, it is in the company . . . and its management and not in the industry that the hypothetical purchaser is likely to be interested". That case concerned a minority shareholding of some 28%.

Share valuation principles require the hypothetical market to be fully open to all potential buyers and this must include the corporate speculator, the institutional buyer and the personal investor. Notwithstanding Danckwerts J's statement (above), if the circumstances of the case—particularly the free availability of information about the company and its prospects—are such that the shares in question can be compared fairly with any quoted company shares, then it is unlikely that the courts would upset a valuation that is fully supported by factual evidence. But otherwise, subject to the following comments, for small minority interests a value based on quoted company comparison is of dubious accuracy at best.

The final word concerning the choice of valuation technique must go to Plowman J in *Re Lynall*. He was considering the various valuation attempts made by expert witnesses in this case which concerned a minority interest in a long-established private company. One witness valued the shares on the basis of a bank injecting money into the company with a view to accelerating expansion and nursing it to the point where the bank itself would be able to float it. The transaction would be one between the board (not an outside shareholder) on the one side and the bank on the other. Plowman J said of this approach "I propose to disregard it"

Assuming that a class of quoted company can be identified, into which can be slotted the subject matter of the valuation, the dividend yields of a number of such companies over a period of, say, three to five years are calculated. The latest dividend yield is calculated by dividing the latest dividend by the latest quoted price (that is, the latest prior to the valuation date) and multiplying by 100; for earlier years one should take the company's year end price.

In this exercise care should be taken to arrive at yields that have been calculated on exactly the same basis. Financial year ends may be different and it is not satisfactory to take published dividend yields that reflect different bases of calculation. Because the published yields are usually based on a calendar year, there is a considerable danger that companies with different financial year ends will be represented quite differently. One company may have paid an interim and a final dividend in respect of that calendar year, whilst another may have paid in that same year a final dividend in respect of a previous financial year and an interim dividend in respect of a financial year not yet completed.

This exercise gives us a range of dividends and dividend yields for a range of companies carrying on business of a similar type or within a similar economic framework. Also, the figures will enable us to calculate the dividend *growth* over the period under review, and it may then be possible to arrive at a required rate of return that includes a dividend growth expectation—if such a rate is wanted for the valuation exercise—but see below. Of the various dividend yields the latest is the most relevant, but a comparison with earlier yields is useful to ensure that the latest is not obviously untypical. If yields have varied considerably over the years, it will be necessary to investigate the reasons—and also perhaps compare that volatility with the movement in money market rates or the FT All Stocks Index.

There are now two further matters to consider:

First, having ascertained the various quoted company dividend yields, can the average of the yields, or any particular one of them be applied to our private company without any further adjustment; and secondly should the dividend growth record be used to influence the yield that is ultimately to be applied?

Tackling the first point is very difficult indeed. There will be an opportunity later in the valuation exercise to discount the share valuation for lack of marketability (see 2.16) and this discount will depend upon many factors, but should discount (or a premium) be applied at this preliminary stage? The answer is to take the "base" yield—ie the quoted company yield—and ask whether that return is reasonable, disregarding the fact that the private company shares lack the readily accessible Stock Exchange market. This question is really determined by reference to the differences between the quoted company and the private company as to security—how long have the respective companies been established, and what is the asset backing (see 6.1); and, secondly, income guarantee—how do the dividend records compare for constancy and stability? The required yield from the private company share would be increased where any required factor was lacking and reduced where there is a surfeit. Similar considerations apply here as apply in the case of discounts from the P/E Ratio—see 5.5.

Secondly, as far as dividend growth is concerned, it is unlikely that any quoted company dividend growth pattern can be used. A dividend growth pattern which is determined directly from the performance of the subject matter of the valuation, whether that is an actual performance or through the notional dividend policy (see 4.6) will be a far better indicator. The quoted company may be useful for determining the current expected rate of return, but only the specific investment itself, ie the private company, can give the promise of future dividends or growth. Therefore, quoted company dividend growth records probably are best used only in establishing a starting point for the current yield, although they may be of some use in making a year-by-year comparison between the quoted company and the private company.

## The alternative

Moving on to the second option, in which quoted securities are ignored altogether, the starting point is to look at the current investment opportunities and consider investment psychology. The purchaser will be someone who has money to invest and is completely free to choose, yet he will choose to acquire the private company shares and these will be purchased not by way of subscription for new shares but by acquisition from the vendor shareholder.

In terms of investment in quoted securities, one would invest with an expectation of income and capital growth. Of course, the stock market can meet most investment requirements—for example some investors require a low income and high capital growth; others require the opposite; some are in for short-term gains, yet others require average income and growth potential to maintain real value against inflation. Some people enjoy the risk-taking, others prefer safety.

As interest rates change, so the value of quoted shares may change and money may move to where a better immediate return is available. If economic problems arise, money may be moved into gilts as a safer prospect for the immediate future—the income yield on gilts is generally on the low side, the risk factor however is also very low. The newest breed of gilt—the index-linked bond—has a very low coupon indeed, but the real value of the investment is protected against the ravages of inflation.

As a general rule the knowing investor will spread his investments for protection and is prepared to take a smaller income yield if his capital is safe—and especially if it is growing. It is unlikely that the average investor will actually risk his capital for a slightly better than average income yield, but he might well put up with inconvenience (such as the inability to convert immediately to cash) to achieve it.

If shares which are being valued on a dividend basis are to be valued without reference to any publicly quoted companies, it may be necessary not only to make projections of dividends (and the earnings out of which they are paid) and value any non-business assets, but also to determine a "risk" factor and an "accessibility" factor.

A free investor may choose to put his money into gilts (possibly for capital gains tax saving purposes), into one or more building societies, into quoted company debentures, local authority loans, savings certificates, single premium bonds or even endowment policies or property. By choosing to ignore quoted company comparisons, a valuer would be relying on far more subjective criteria in determining his value, effectively entering a much wider and competitive investment market. That market will require a much higher yield from a minority interest in a private company than it would from the traditional forms of investment—except where the private company's asset-backing or earnings factor is sufficiently strong to justify a lower yield. The effect of these matters on the required yield can be substantial. In cases where the asset-backing is stronger than is necessary simply to contribute towards maintaining dividends it might be proper not only to look at a dividend yield basis of valuation but also at whether an asset-basis valuation would be appropriate. An investment company or property company may be cases where an asset-related value or a hybrid basis is more appropriate than a dividend yield basis. It may still be, of course, that the asset valuation would be heavily discounted for a minority interest. Alternatively, perhaps the earnings of the business are too great to be ignored, and an earnings basis should also be taken into account. The combination of valuation bases is dealt with in Chapter 7.

If the other valuation bases cannot displace the dividend yield, it is necessary to identify how secure the investment is and how easily accessible it would be. For example, would the bank accept the shares as security for an overdraft facility or other borrowing and upon what terms, and how would that compare with alternative investments. Looking at the company itself and the shareholding in question, how do the prospects for future income and future capital growth compare with the alternative investments available? Does the projected maintainable dividend or earnings yield compare favourably or unfavourably with the current yield on, say, undated gilts, bank deposit interest or more sophisticated money market returns? Do the alternative investment opportunities that equate with the income yield from the shares also equate with the capital growth expectations from the shares, or *vice versa*. By building up a picture of the comparative pros and cons, a required yield can be determined; and this is where the art of the valuer is tested in the extreme.

The advent of the index-linked gilts has provided the investor with a thoroughly safe, long-term, investment medium. It is not a short-term prospect because so much of the yield is stored up to accrue at maturity, and the coupon is extremely low because the value of the capital is protected against inflation. There is also the benefit that capital gains from gilt-edged securities (and qualifying corporate bonds—see Finance Act 1984 s.64 and Finance Act 1985 s.67) are free of tax. After 1 July 1986 there is no longer the requirement to hold these securities and bonds for 12 months to qualify for the exemption.

But it is unlikely that these securities can be of any direct use in helping to establish a required yield for private company shares. Their average gross redemption yield is smaller than non-index-linked gilts by a factor of 3 and this yield will be directly affected by the rate of inflation, which is unlikely in the case of yields from ordinary shares.

A tool that may be used to identify how secure the dividends are is the dividend cover. This is the number of times that the current dividend yield could be met out of current net profits. It is not an absolute measure, because there are many factors which can affect the level of dividends, but, for example, a low cover (of 1 or 1.5) would indicate no profit retention in the business. This would be acceptable, for example, if the company was not carrying on a business that requires capital expenditure or cash retention. A high cover, of above 4, would be acceptable if the company does require to invest back into its business.

A look at the past few years' dividend cover record may prove useful in checking the company's consistency; it may also be helpful in identifying whether the shareholders' dividends are hard-earned or otherwise. Where a comparison is being made with a quoted company, the dividend cover may also be compared, as this is one of the data published in the Financial Times.

Even if a comparison with quoted equity shares is not being made, it may nevertheless be helpful to look at the general level of yields for the particular industry as a whole. The Exchange Telegraph Cards (via the Actuaries Share Indices (FTASI)) will give the yield for some of the larger companies in various industries—but in view of the size and make-up of those companies the yields may be considerably smaller than might be expected from a small or medium sized private company.

The Shares Valuation Division in their assessment of the share value may start from one of the following arbitrary values and develop from there:

(a) for companies with a net asset value greater than £500,000 the dividend yield is the FTASI rate plus 50%—but above this level it is unlikely that the SVD will concede that a value could be arrived at without reference to direct quoted company comparisons;

(b) for net asset values between £150,000 and £500,000, a yield of twice the FTASI would be a starting point;

(c) for smaller companies, a current dividend yield might be 12.5% to 15%, and an earnings yield might be 35% to 40%, or up to 50% if no dividend is being paid.

## 4.9 Distribution regulation

It may be that a minimum level of distribution is required by law such as at present in the UK for close companies with a certain level of investment income (Finance Act 1972 s.94 and Sch. 16). Indeed, in some countries distributions are restricted, for example until the company's shareholders' reserves as shown on the balance sheet reach a specified level, possibly fixed by reference to net creditors, loan capital and so on.

The current law regarding State dividend regulation must be examined at the time of the valuation, and its impact on future distributions is an important factor in determining the likelihood of maintaining the current distributions in the future. The fact that the directors of the company would not pay dividends were it not for a legal requirement is no reason to value a minority shareholding on the basis that no dividends would be paid given a freely determined dividend policy. It may be possible to argue that the entitlement to dividends under some legal regulation is more precarious than if distributions were made as a conscious decision by the company, and thus the value of the "forced" dividend may be (but is not invariably) less than a "planned" dividend.

Unless some clear indication of a change in the law exists it must be supposed that the regulation, whatever it may be, will continue into the future. It would be reasonable to look at the history of the law in question as this may indicate how permanent it is likely to be. For example, the present "apportionment rules" which penalise a close company which has non-trading income for not declaring a certain level of distribution evolved from earlier "shortfall" legislation which was, in fact, more demanding. At the time of writing, it would be unreasonable to assume that the apportionment rules will be further relaxed in the foreseeable future. Indeed, a change of government might see the introduction of a more demanding regime. On the other hand, it is not impossible for there to be a dividend freeze.

If, despite the apportionment rules dividends are not being declared, the company will suffer certain tax penalties, and the minority shareholders will not receive any dividend income. The appropriate valuation will be made on that basis, but it may be worthwhile considering whether an action for oppression of minority interests could be contemplated by the minority shareholders. If so, the valuation should assume that the dividends would be paid.

# Chapter 5

# The earnings basis

## 5.1 Shareholding influence

The earnings basis is normally appropriate for the valuation of a majority shareholding in a company that will not be liquidated in the foreseeable future—ie it is a going concern. The earnings basis looks at the future profit-generating potential of the company—the post-tax profits available for distribution after interest and preference dividends are paid. Thus, the valuer seeks to establish the maintainable profits (which are the profits that, on the evidence, can be maintained, all other things being equal, in the future). This profit figure is then capitalised, inflation and growth factors being considered, to give the present day worth of the right to receive those future earnings.

It will be realised that the payment of ordinary dividends out of current profits and reserves will depend upon the company's dividend policy. That policy will have the approval of the majority shareholders but minority shareholders will generally have no power individually to influence the payment of dividends. So a single majority shareholder, because of his power over the distribution of the company's profits, has a more valuable asset than an equivalent, aggregated, shareholding made up of individual minority shareholdings. That value is not based on a mere "hope" or "expectation" of dividends but on the certain ability (subject only to commercial factors) of the majority shareholder to turn current profits and available reserves to his individual advantage whenever he so chooses.

Thus, a majority shareholder's interest in a company will normally be valued on an "earnings" basis, the "dividend basis" being more appropriate for minority interests (see Chapter 4).

The assets basis (see Chapter 6) does not usually apply because the value of the business assets is reflected automatically in the earnings. The distributable profits (the earnings) are derived from net operating profits. Net operating profits are before tax and before payment of debenture interest and preference dividends and these profits are derived from the employment of the *assets* in the business—whether fixed assets, cash, goodwill or any other asset. Provided the capitalised value of the post-tax profits is equal to or greater than the post-tax value of the business assets, the value of those assets is fully reflected in the annual profits. The impact of tax on the distributable profits is discussed below.

Of course, most rules are subject to some qualification, and in this context a separate valuation of assets may certainly be necessary if there are assets standing to one side of the business assets and which have an independent value in their own right. In such a case, the earnings basis would only deal with part of the story and an asset valuation may be necessary to complete it. Again, in the case of impending liquidation, neither an earnings basis nor a dividend basis would be appropriate as there would be no earnings or income distributions in prospect (even if there had previously been a full dividend-paying policy), but only capital distribution of cash or kind.

Finally, in some cases it may be appropriate to take a mixture of valuation bases, giving each basis a weighting as against the others; see Chapter 7.

## 5.2 Earnings

Although Statement of Standard Accounting Practice No 3 (Earnings per Share) (published by the Institute of Chartered Accountants in England and Wales) is not intended to apply to the majority of unlisted companies, it nevertheless contains useful assistance. Earnings can be defined by reference to the definition of "Earnings per share" thus:

> "the profit-in-pence attributable to each equity share, based on the *consolidated profit of the period after tax and after deducting minority interests and preference dividends, but before taking into account extraordinary items*, divided by the number of equity shares in issue and ranking for dividend in respect of the period."

Using this definition then the annual earnings of the company can be extracted from the company's accounts. There remains the question of the place of taxation and there are currently three ways of calculating earnings having regard to the impact of taxation on profit and distributions: the gross basis; the net basis; and the nil basis.

The *gross basis* recognises that when a distribution is made out of a company's profits advance corporation tax (ACT) of (assuming a basic rate of 30%) 3/7ths is paid to the Inland Revenue, and within limits, this ACT is credited against the mainstream corporation tax that the company bears on the profits out of which the distribution is paid. The ACT is also a tax credit (at the basic rate of income tax) for the UK resident recipient of the distribution. For example, if a company made profits after mainstream corporation tax at 35%, of £550, it would be able to make a distribution of that amount to its shareholders who would be treated as having received £786 and would be entitled to a tax credit of £236 (ie 3/7ths of £550). Therefore the gross earnings of individual taxpayers may be said to be not the post-corporation tax profits of £550, but the gross pre-tax value of £786.

There are complications to this, because if the basic rate of tax changed to, say, 35%, the gross pre-tax value would become

$$£550 \times \frac{100)}{65} = £846,$$

and if it fell to 25% would become

$$£550 \times \frac{100}{75} = £733$$

So the gross earnings can be affected by a change in the tax rate, which, of course, has little or nothing to do with the company's performance. Franked investment income (ie dividends having suffered ACT) will not be further taxed in the hands of a recipient company and the tax credit can be set against ACT which is payable in respect of distributions made by the recipient company itself.

It is unlikely (except in the case of investment companies subject to dividend regulation) that any company would distribute its entire distributable earnings—an estimate of a reasonable annual distribution policy for a trading company would be 25% of (pre-tax) distributable profits.

On the basis that earnings and assets are valued in net of tax terms, thereby treating tax as an expense, the gross basis is unlikely to be of use in calculating the earnings that are to be capitalised. For the dividend basis, however, because it is the pure income stream with attendant tax credit that is being valued, the tendency is to capitalise the gross dividend yield and that would mean grossing-up the yield for the ACT/tax credit.

The *nil basis* is the basis often used in determining earnings. It is simply the post-mainstream corporation tax profits and as such reflects the net value to the shareholder after net corporation tax plus basic rate tax.

The *net basis* considers a special problem where the mainstream corporation tax charge is small (because, eg, the company has a large double tax credit relief), but the ACT charge is high because of a full distribution policy. In this case the "surplus" ACT that could not be set against mainstream corporation tax liability and the corporation tax liability itself are together deducted from gross profits.

The PE ratios quoted in the Financial Times Actuaries Share Index are on the net and the nil bases.

### Pre 1973 Basis

There were fundamental changes in the basis of taxation of companies in April 1965 and April 1973 and it is not possible to make precise comparisons of earnings under the different bases although it is unlikely that such a comparison would be necessary except for valuations on dates within five to ten years of April 1965 and April 1973.

## 5.3 The valuation approach

There are two ways of arriving at an earnings-based value:

- price-earnings ratio basis
- required yield basis

One or other basis may be chosen because it gives a more "acceptable" value according to the purpose for which valuation is undertaken; because of a personal preference for that particular method; or because supporting evidence for a valuation is not available to allow the other basis to be used. However, the first basis, by reference to the Price to Earnings ratio automatically brings into the exercise a comparison with quoted companies because the Price to Earnings ratio is a factor that is relevant to the performance of companies, as will be seen.

The required yield basis suffers the difficulty of defining feasible alternative investments and this has been covered in some detail in Chapter 4.

## 5.4 Price-Earnings Ratio Basis—the quoted company comparison

The Price-Earnings ratio (PER) is basically a capitalisation factor to translate earnings into a current purchase value. It is really another way of expressing the required yield but is determined in a somewhat different fashion. Suppose the PER is 8 and the current earnings (after tax) are £100,000. The value of those earnings in current purchasing terms would be 8 × 100,000 = £800,000. This capitalised value may be subject to adjustment as explained later in this Chapter.

It would be simple to take the earnings per share as

calculated according to SSAP 3 (see 5.2 above) and apply a PER ratio to give an immediate current valuation of that share. Unfortunately there are one or two practical difficulties.

First, it should be explained that a PER is not something that can be defined absolutely. Its only real value for valuation purposes is as a "constant" which can be applied to the earnings in order to give a value. That would be acceptable if, indeed, a constant value could be identified.

The Inland Revenue relies heavily on PERs, and is unlikely to alter its approach in the foreseeable future. The major objections to PERs are that the ratios used by the Inland Revenue are those for publicly quoted companies, which exist in an economic sector quite distinct from that of the private company.

In looking at PERs of "comparable" public quoted companies, adjustments may be necessary, usually by watering down the "quoted" PER, to remove special factors, such as particularly strong asset-backing, or shares being in great demand perhaps because of personal attributes of the chief executive (say, a public figure), or earnings are based on diversified activities.

The list of peculiarities is endless and it is therefore necessary to take a good number of "comparable" companies and look towards identifying an acceptable average PER that could be appropriate for the private company if its shares were for sale in the quoted company market. That PER should then be adjusted (usually downwards) to remove the quoted company characteristics that the subject private company lacks (see 5.5). Having determined a revised PER and having calculated a value, that value should then be discounted for lack of marketability because, of course, the private company is *not* in the quoted company market and it therefore lacks the benefits of being in that market, and usually suffers the problem of pre-emption restrictions (see 2.13). The starting point for this discount will be 35% but subject to negotiation up or down—see 2.16.

Despite these misgivings, the PER of public quoted

companies *is* relevant if only because for fiscal purposes the Inland Revenue will usually value by reference to it. But it has also to be said that the PER for publicly quoted companies provides a starting point which can be very useful, provided the differences between the two types of company are not lost and, indeed, are specifically identified and catered for.

The Revenue regard the PER as an expression of the degree of the market's confidence that any given company can maintain its earnings and its growth in the future. In making quoted company comparisons the SVD does seek to identify comparable companies and should not include any that are clearly out of step. Some of the faces of unacceptable comparison are mentioned above, and companies which are in the throes of public discussion should probably be excluded; so too would be shares recently suspended by the Council of the Stock Exchange. The inclusion of shares which have been ignored by the market should be questioned, so too should any company whose shares alone have been showing a continual decline in price. In the full range of "comparable" companies the very best and the very worst performers should be removed altogether from the choice of which to take on board to construct the average PER ratio. The number of companies to be taken is as many as one can practicably justify being comparable within acceptable tolerances. Naturally, this means that care must be taken first to compare like with like. If the private company is heavy engineering it would not be appropriate to compare companies in any industry outside heavy engineering—unless some special factor was present. If the main function of the company in question is to provide transport services, even if exclusively within the industry, it may be necessary to look at quoted transport companies because only they would have comparable underlying economics—except, of course, that the subject company's fortunes may vary in direct relationship with that of the heavy engineering sector. Thus, it may be necessary to start by taking a compromise between the PER for the heavy engineering sector and that for the transport sector. This would in turn depend upon the influence that the fortunes of one sector of the economy can be shown to have on the profits of the subject company.

Other factors that affect the like-with-like approach are:

*Geographical:* The quality of earnings may certainly be affected by where those earnings arise; currency movements and local exchange controls will often affect the clean repatriation of full earnings. A valuable asset base built up in a far-off land, and which owes itself solely to the local restriction on removal of profits may not seem quite as valuable in the UK. On the other hand a strong export base is likely to give a company a better outlook than a company dependent upon a restricted home market, but possibly with an attendant currency exposure.

*Debt/Equity:* The ratio of debt to equity will certainly be of influence in price-fixing. An imbalance of debt may mean the company is paying a higher interest charge than other comparable companies and the current level of interest rates—or perhaps more important the future expected level of interest rates—will influence the share price.

*Market fashion:* If, for example, computers are "in" or "out", or leisure centres are "in" or "out" of fashion at any time, the value of shares in those quoted favoured or unfavoured sectors may be markedly affected though it may well be a very short-term phenomenon. It may be that the subject company can also enjoy the fruits of this fashion, or must expect the same disadvantages, but if it can be argued successfully that the phenomenon is short-lived and can only affect quoted shares—ie it is a characteristic of the stock market itself—then the fashion factor can be side-stepped. A three year average of PERs may be more accurate. Where a company may be influenced by two separate prime sectors of the economy it is particularly important that any fashion factor affecting one sector should be excluded.

A final point for consideration in making stock market comparisons is the timing of the comparison. If company results are expected, the price is likely to be up or down depending upon expectations.

## 5.5 Discounts from and adjustments to the quoted PER

Notwithstanding all efforts to identify "comparable" companies and determine a reasonable average PER, the various problem areas already mentioned must be taken into account. This may be done by discounting the PER. The discount for lack of marketability (2.16) is normally taken into account at the final stages of share valuation, but the quoted PER itself may be discounted for lack of management expertise (if that can be shown) by possibly 10%. For disparity in intrinsic strength and resilience, which may be manifest in the capital structure, diversification (or lack of it), proven or unproven track record and so on, higher discounts may be in order. If it is felt that discounts beyond, say, 30% should be taken, it is probable that the "comparable" companies are not really comparable at all and perhaps further enquiry is necessary to establish the proper PER; or perhaps the alternative required yield basis should be considered. For investment companies, see 2.16.

Finally, one of the major differences between unquoted and quoted shares is the market place for each, and another common difference, though not universal, is the size and financial sophistication of the quoted company compared to its smaller, unquoted cousin. When these two factors combine, the quoted share will usually have a volatility in its market that the unquoted company share will not have. The quoted company's volatility is called "beta" and 1.0 is the normal beta. A beta greater than 1.0 (say 1.3) indicates that if there is a movement in the market as a whole the share price will respond by moving at a faster rate in that same direction by the same factor as the beta bears to 1.0; thus a 10% movement in a market would cause a 13% movement in the particular share price, up or down.

In making a quoted share comparison with private company shares, one would be justified in identifying the betas of the companies taken for comparison purposes, in order to note that the yields and the PERs in respect of those shares with high betas relate to more volatile stock.

The "defensive" shares with betas of 1.0 and below are not volatile and consequently, all other things being equal, their yields would be lower than their volatile counterparts. In the right circumstances, the valuer may adjust the average yield or PER from the quoted company shares to take into account any high beta factors that are included in his list of quoted companies.

## 5.6 The required yield basis

By ignoring a quoted company comparison, the capitalisation of future maintainable profits must be by reference to a required yield. This is discussed, in relation to the dividend basis, at 4.8.

The SVD view is that if it is not possible to find comparable quoted companies the average yield for the appropriate industry as shown, for example, in the FT Actuaries Share Indices which is published in the Financial Times, is to be taken. Because the companies whose performances are taken into the FTASI are large and the yields heavily biased towards blue-chip companies, SVD will generally not take issue with an adjustment to reflect the differences of size, vulnerability, expertise, etc between the private company and the FTASI. This, however, only goes to prove how unsatisfactory the "official" indices are—in the same way as is direct quoted company comparison.

At a practical level, the required yield will not be less than the yield available from index-linked gilts and probably will not be less than unindexed gilts. In view of the fact that gilts are now free of capital gains tax irrespective of how long they are held, this minimum yield for private company comparison should probably be increased by 50% to compensate for the tax disadvantage alone.

For small companies, say with value no more than £200,000 a yield of around 50% may be appropriate; a lower yield would be appropriate if dividends are being paid. Above that value the yield will fall and an average of around 30—35% may be expected. Much depends on the facts of the case: the condition of the company, its management and the economic climate.

It may be argued that the potential investor in private company shares chooses that form of investment in preference to the alternatives because he is some special sort of investor. However, he will be taking the decision in the full knowledge of the alternatives available to him and he would be most unwise to invest in a private company without expecting to make his money work for him no less effectively than if it was placed elsewhere. If the immediate income to be derived from the holding is paltry then he would expect to make up the difference either by personal involvement in the business of the company or because of the longer term prospects for growth. For valuation purposes, the former is to be ignored: it is a personal reason that would be absent from the rest of the market and is not commercially valuable, unless, in the circumstances of the case, that particular purchaser is recognised as a "special purchaser", but not one influenced by personal reasons (2.11).

The required rate of return should therefore be weighted by the growth factor that can be discerned from the company's results and all the surrounding circumstances. The formula for this exercise is given, in relation to dividend basis valuation, at 4.8.

## 5.7 Capitalising the earnings

Given the PER or the required yield the next step is to apply it to the company's earnings. The earnings for the last or the current year are not satisfactory in isolation because the exercise is to capitalise the future maintainable earnings and the current year's profits are no more than one element pointing towards what that figure may be. Several years should be examined to discern the profit (or loss) trend, the impact of inflation, and the measure of growth. The purpose is to identify an inflation-free amount in today's value of tomorrow's promised profit, profit that one can be fairly certain will be maintained. There may be a good chance that those promised profits will be exceeded in the future, but equally there will be some risk that they will not be reached. Over-optimism is to be avoided, in favour of a sane and rational view of the level of maintainable profits that the company can generate without any significant change in the *status quo*. One method of measuring such earnings can be found in the weighted average model, which looks at the results of the past five or so years as adjusted for inflation to give today's values, taking the average of those values (using the "sum of the digits" basis) and adjusting the average for expected growth.

In this model it is important to reflect properly the impact of cyclical profitability: if, for example, only one half of a cyclical trend is incorporated the result is likely to be out of proportion to reality. A cyclical trend may also have a marked effect on the growth factor to be introduced. In cases of fluctuating earnings apart from cyclical trends, it may help to smooth the model if the highest and lowest results (after adjusting for inflation) are removed from the calculation of the weighted average.

In the following examples figures are rounded for convenience:

*Example:*

| Year ended 30 April | Profits (losses) | RPI at 30 April | Profits (losses) adjusted to 1985 values | Result taken for model | |
|---|---|---|---|---|---|
| 1978 | (52,000) | 195 | (100,000) × | | |
| 1979 | 100,000 | 214 | 175,000 | 175,000 × 1 | 175,000 |
| 1980 | 110,000 | 261 | 158,000 | 158,000 × 2 | 316,000 |
| 1981 | 140,000 | 292 | 180,000 | 180,000 × 3 | 540,000 |
| 1982 | 175,000 | 320 | 205,000 × | | |
| 1983 | 180,000 | 332 | 203,000 | 203,000 × 4 | 812,000 |
| 1984 | 190,000 | 350 | 203,000 | 203,000 × 5 | 1,015,000 |
| 1985 | 195,000 | 374 | 195,000 | 195,000 × 6 | 1,170,000 |
| | | | 1,219,000 | 21 | 4,028,000 |

Weighted average $\dfrac{4,028,000}{21}$ (say) = 192,000

*Comparison notes*
1. The arithmetical mean over the 8 years is 1,219,000 divided by 8 = 152,000

2. The arithmetical mean over the last 5 years is 986,000 divided by 5 = <u>197,000</u>
3. The full weighted average over the 8 years (ie not excluding any results) is 6,668,000 divided by 36 = <u>185,000</u>
4. A full weighted average over the last 5 years is 2,986,000 divided by 15 = <u>199,000</u>.

In this example, in adjusting for inflation, a not untypical situation has arisen. A smooth profit trend has been turned into a fluctuating series but one that also shows a declining profit trend. Problems arise particularly as to whether any growth factor should be introduced, and if so the quantum. The weighted average of £192,000 seems to be a reasonable expression of what could be regarded as future maintainable profits at today's prices.

It might be argued that simple extrapolation of the unadjusted profits would suggest that in 1986 profits would be in the order of £200,000—£205,000. How can a mere £192,000 be justified? The answer is that the 1986 profits must be looked at *after* adjustment for inflation, otherwise like is not being compared with like. If the 1986 RPI is likely to be somewhere between 390 and 404, it is reasonable to take 398. £205,000 at an RPI of 398, adjusted to today's prices of 374 is £192,638, so it appears that £192,000 is about right.

If this is still not convincing, the RPI adjusted profit-growth comparisons should be examined. For this purpose, two comparisons are given, the first comparison is between one year's profits and those for the earliest year showing profits—ie 1979; and the second is between one year's profits and those for the previous year.

## Growth comparisons

| Year | Profit £'000 | RPI | Adjusted to 1985 values | % Increase on 1979 | on previous year | |
|------|------|------|------|------|------|------|
| 1979 | 100 | 214 | 175 | — | — | |
| 1980 | 110 | 261 | 158 | (−10%) | (−10%) | |
| 1981 | 140 | 292 | 180 | 3% | 14% | |
| 1982 | 175 | 320 | 205 | 17% | 14% | |
| 1983 | 180 | 332 | 203 | 16% | (−1%) | |
| 1984 | 190 | 350 | 203 | 16% | 0 | |
| 1985 | 195 | 374 | 195 | 11% | (−4%) | |
| 1986 | 200 | 398 | 187 | 7% | (−4%) | (a) £187,000 |
| | 205 | 398 | 193 | 10% | (−1%) | (b) £193,000 |
| | 210 | 398 | 197 | 13% | 1% | (c) £197,000 |

Which result is to be taken for 1986—(a), (b) or (c)? Whatever figure is taken, no additional growth factor should be taken into account. The figure would represent the maintainable pre-tax profits of the company and the appropriate PER or yield would be applied to it after corporation tax is deducted.

But, past performance can only be one of the factors in determining a reasonable level of maintainable profits.

## Cyclical trend

If a cyclical trend is present, this must be reflected in the future maintainable profits if it is not reflected in the PER. It is important to ensure that the effect of a cyclical trend is not missed, but neither should its effect be incorporated more than once. Cycles may be short or long.

If short—say 3 to 5 years—it would give rise to considerable inaccuracies unless the earnings model ranges well beyond one cycle. Even so, it is important to identify when, within that cycle, the valuation date falls. This will assist in deciding which end of a range of possible earnings should be chosen as the maintainable profits. Thus, looking at the previous example, if it could be shown that a five-year cyclical business has bottomed-out and a growth rate comparable to 1982 is likely, the future maintainable profits may be determined as (c) or greater (but probably greater only if the periodic growth rate is proven by earlier cycles). On the other hand, if the cycle has peaked (say in 1982) and will not bottom out for two or three years the future maintainable profits may not exceed (a) or less. Great care must be taken where cyclical business is involved: a change of product, management, location or fashion may destroy cyclical business and appropriate caution—and enquiry—is necessary. Long term cyclical business is even more difficult to deal with because a longer period for comparison of profits, growth etc is needed. It could be argued that rather than fine-tune maintainable profits by reference to cycles greater than, say, ten years, the PER or yield should be adjusted. Quoted company PERs may indeed reflect cyclical business in appropriate cases.

## Linear trend analysis

Another statistical model that may be of some assistance to the valuer is the linear trend analysis model where the object is to take a series and smoothe it into a steady pattern. But it does not always provide a helpful answer. The future year's profit is given by solving the simultaneous equation:

$$\varepsilon(y) = na + \varepsilon(x)b$$
$$\varepsilon(xy) = \varepsilon(x)a + \varepsilon(x^2)b$$

Hopefully, for the less mathematically minded, the following example can, with a little patience, be followed through:

| % growth of "y" profits on previous year | Year ended 30 Ap. | Profit | RPI at 30 April | Profit adjusted to 1985 values (y) | (x) | (xy) | $(x^2)$ (a) | (b) |
|---|---|---|---|---|---|---|---|---|
| | 1978 | 78,000 | 195 | 150,000 | x 1 | 150,000 | 1 | 85,608 + 1 (35,726) = 121,334 |
| +10% | 1979 | 94,500 | 214 | 165,000 | x 2 | 330,000 | 4 | 85,608 + 2 (35,726) = 157,060 |
| +12% | 1980 | 129,000 | 261 | 185,000 | x 3 | 555,000 | 9 | 85,608 + 3 (35,726) = 192,786 |
| +12.5% | 1981 | 162,000 | 292 | 208,000 | x 4 | 832,000 | 16 | 85,608 + 4 (35,726) = 228,512 |
| +12.5% | 1982 | 200,000 | 320 | 234,000 | x 5 | 1,170,000 | 25 | 85,608 + 5 (35,726) = 264,238 |
| +20% | 1983 | 249,000 | 332 | 281,000 | x 6 | 1,686,000 | 36 | 85,608 + 6 (35,726) = 299,964 |
| + 20% | 1984 | 315,000 | 350 | 337,000 | x 7 | 2,359,000 | 49 | 85,608 + 7 (35,726) = 335,690 |
| +22% | 1985 | 411,000 | 374 | 411,000 | x 8 | 3,288,000 | 64 | 85,608 + 8 (35,726) = 371,416 |
| | | | | 1,971,000 | 36 | 10,370,000 | 204 | 1,971,000 |

n is the number of years in the model. $\varepsilon$ means "the sum of"

(1)  ... $\varepsilon(y) = na + \varepsilon(x)b$
(2)  ... $\varepsilon(xy) = \varepsilon(x) a + \varepsilon(x^2) b$

Substituting =

(1)  ... 1,971,000 = 8a + 36b
(2)  ... 10,370,000 = 36a + 204b

Multiplying (1) by 9 and (2) by 2 =
(3)  ... 17,739,000 = 72a + 324b
(4)  ... 20,740,000 = 72a + 408b

Subtracting (3) from (4) =
(5)  ..: 3,001,000 = 84b
Therefore b = 35,726

Substituting in (3)
(6)  ... 17,739,000 = 72a + 11,575,224
Therefore a = 85,608

Extrapolating for 1986: 371,416 + 35,726 = £407,142

This is less than 1985, and with the recent RPI adjusted profit growth rates proven by performance (1983 — 20%, 1984 — 20% and 1985 — 22%) it is unlikely that anyone would really expect, merely on the profit trend, that 1986 would be a lesser figure — more likely somewhere in the region of 411,000 + 20% = 493,000, or 411,000 + 22% = 501,000.

Linear trend analysis of the years 1983, 1984 and 1985 alone gives an extrapolated 1986 profit of 473,000. This would appear to be the minimum maintainable level of future profits and represents a growth rate of 15%. It may take pretty hard evidence to prove that a 20-22% growth rate could be achieved, but if the evidence is available it could quite easily take precedence over the figures thrown up by statistical models. This particular example of linear trend analysis shows that with strong, persistent growth the model does not truly reflect reality. However, if those profits were uneven and a simple forward extrapolation not possible, the linear trend model would provide a straight line of best fit and a future trend in keeping (within the overall growth rate) with past performance.

# Chapter 6

# The assets basis

## 6.1 Asset-backing

Apart from cases where the liquidation of the company is imminent, the open market value of the assets belonging to a company would normally only figure in a valuation exercise if the company's asset-backing (that is the net realisable value of the company's assets) is greater than the capitalised value of dividends and earnings. It is not possible to give a rule of thumb on this because circumstances vary so. For example, two companies, A and B, each pay the same dividends and enjoy the same level of earnings (and, all other things being equal, both parties' shares would be valued on a dividend or earnings basis at the same price). A's net realisable asset value is negligible and B's net realisable value upon a liquidation would equal the company's value on a going-concern basis. An investment in B's shares appears to carry very little risk and to be easier to sell at a future time than A's shares. That asset-backing must influence the share price and therefore the company's assets and liabilities must be valued and reflected in the "going-concern" valuation.

This is an instance of the net asset value influencing a share price. There are situations where the net asset value, or "break-up" value, will itself be the basis for valuation instead of either the dividend or earnings basis.

In *Attorney-General of Ceylon* v *Mackie*, Lord Reid said "If it is proved in a particular case that at the relevant date the business could not have been sold for more than the value of its tangible assets, then that must be taken to be its value as a *going concern*". That is not to say that the business is *deemed* to be a going concern, but a going concern business cannot necessarily be regarded as worth more than the value of its assets.

## 6.2 Alternative bases

An important point to keep in mind in an asset valuation is that there are several different asset-bases:

*Straight net asset basis*

This is the full current market value (not necessarily the book value on the balance sheet) of business or non-business assets within the company, and this basis is adopted when it is not expected or necessary to realise the assets. Normally the assets would be expected to increase in value because they will remain within the company and the company will continue its business, or at least not be liquidated in the foreseeable future; see Chapter 7. It is necessary to separate out those assets which contribute to the company's earnings because their value will automatically have been reflected in the value of capitalised earnings.

*Break-up basis*

This is the value that would be realised upon the liquidation of the company and the sale of assets and stock, collection of debts and so on. The full market value for each asset (not necessarily the balance sheet value) is ascertained and this value must then be discounted by an element for loss on or cost of realisation. For example, upon a liquidation of a trading company, to get in all the debts within a reasonable period of time — say 30 days or even 60 days — it may be realistic to accept that at least 5% or 10% of these debtors may not pay — and that it would not be economical after a certain period to pursue them. Alternatively, the entire debtor list may be sold to a debt factoring agency, or debt collectors used. Stock and work-in-progress more often than not consists of perishables and "wasted" work that cannot be realised upon a liquidation. A much higher discount may be necessary in these cases — often 50%, but depending upon the nature of the items. Additionally, the valuer must take into account possible redundancy pay and compensation; a provision of at least 10% of the annual staff costs would be a prudent move — but a precise cost can often be determined. The early repayment of loans may carry a penalty, as may the cancellation of a lease. Short-term leaseholds may have a balance-sheet value but may in fact be impossible to assign, not to mention possible dilapidation liabilities and deferred tax charges (basically the claw-back of capital allowances on a discontinuance of trade or disposal of cars, plant, machinery or industrial buildings).

Because the purpose is to value the shares, not the individual assets, the question is what would someone pay to take over all these assets so that he can sell them out of the company and then liquidate the company and take the money remaining? On the break-up basis we have to take into account the asset-stripper's profit. In *Re Courthorpe*, the Court accepted that a shareholder who did not have control but who *might* have been able to compel a winding-up would want a 50% profit — ie a one-third discount from the realisable value of the assets. The profit mark-up is unlikely to change significantly where the majority of the shares are for sale, unless it can be shown that the assets are readily saleable, in which case one might argue down to 30% profit or a 23% discount, perhaps less in some cases. The possibility of a special purchaser should not be forgotten.

*Forced-sale basis*

This falls within the break-up basis but is a rather more serious version of it. It may be evident that at the date of valuation the only way to realise any value from the assets of the company would be to dispose of them within a limited time. This basis more usually applies where to delay the disposal will actually cost more than to sell at an unusually large discount and the obvious example is where funding costs are exceptionally high, the interest rate is high and there are no or insufficient earnings from which to meet the interest charge. Suppose a loan of £100,000 at a real rate of interest of 30% has been made to a company and the loan is secured on a factory valued at £150,000. There are no earnings as the business has just collapsed. The property's full value may only be realised after is has been on the market for 6 to 12 months, yet the interest cost over 12 months will be £30,000. On top of this the lender may be able to take possession of the property, sell it at any price above £100,000 and return the net proceeds after costs of disposal, legal fees, interest unpaid, etc. All in all it may be better to dispose of the factory with least possible delay, and this may require an immediate and heavy discount from the current market value.

Additionally, in this case, whatever is in or around the factory that constitutes separate stock or assets would have to be disposed of before the new tenant takes up occupation: a further forced sale at "knock-down" prices. In the case of leased property, it may be a condition of giving up the lease that the premises are completely vacated — and this may mean that rather than any realisation of assets on the premises, there are costs of removal, dumping or storage.

## 6.3 Taxation

Having determined a valuation for the assets the next matter to consider is the effect of taxation. So far as the realisation of stock and work in progress is concerned this would only give rise to a corporation tax charge if sold at a price above the balance sheet provision. Plant and machinery disposed of below its tax written-down value would create a further tax allowance (which may or may not be utilisable against current or past profits, depending upon a variety of factors). If sold at above that value, the sale would create a balancing charge and if, as is unlikely, it is sold above its original cost, it may in some circumstances give rise to a chargeable gain.

On the basis of a break-up or forced sale the resultant tax

charge must be brought into account in the share valuation, for it is the net of tax charge that the liquidating shareholder would be able to realise outside the company (but no account would be taken of post-liquidation taxation outside the company).

In the case of the straight net-asset basis the underlying capital gains tax liability would not be taken into the net value calculation if disposal is not being contemplated. It may not be unreasonable, however, to allow a discount from the full value to recognise the latent liability should a disposal be made within, say, three to five years. This discount very largely depends upon the full facts of the case, and particularly the economic benefit that would accrue to a purchaser of the shares if he had power to dispose of the asset. An example of the impact of corporation tax on a company's chargeable gains is given in Chapter 7.

Tax problems may be encountered, in relation to real property, under Taxes Act 1970 s.488 and generally, under Taxes Act 1970 s.460. Where groups of companies are concerned Taxes Act 1970 s.267 may be relevant. Indeed, the tax consequences of any disposal arrangement should be considered, and to the extent that they could have an impact within the company in a real sale, it may be appropriate to reflect that impact in a deduction from net asset value.

## 6.4 Precedence of asset-basis

In summary, the principal situations where the assets basis takes precedence over other bases are:

(i) where a company is in liquidation or about to go into liquidation. In *Re Courthorpe* it was shown that a heavy discount on the value of the company's shares would be in order (one-third in this case) where the motive behind the acquisition of the shares is to liquidate the company and take a profit on the sale of the company's assets. It will be realised that in calculating the present value of the shares (ie before this discount) the costs of disposing of the assets and the discounted value of the assets on a break-up basis will already have been taken into account;

(ii) where the asset-backing is substantially under-utilised and there is no prospect of improving the profitability of the company's current activities. In *M'Connel's Trustees* v *IRC*, the company made a loss in each of the three years after its formation and there was never any prospect of the company earning profits or being in a position to pay a dividend. Lord Fleming held that the holder of the company's shares would be in a position to put the company into voluntary liquidation and to realise the whole assets and divide the value thereof amongst the shareholders;

(iii) where the assets stand to one side of the business and have a value in their own right;

(iv) in the special case of investment etc holding companies (see 6.5 below).

### Minority shareholders

In the event of impending liquidation the minority share-holder will be entitled to a *pro rata* share of the net asset value. This would not be the case in other asset based valuations where the value would therefore have to be discounted because the minority shareholder's entitle-ment would only be on paper. The amount of the discount depends upon the size of the minority holding, the "quality" of the asset backing and the likelihood of the value being realised. Shareholdings of less than 10% might be discounted by 50% or more (before any discount for lack of marketability) (and see 6.5). This matter is more fully discussed in the Example in 7.4.

## 6.5 Investment etc holding companies

In the case of a company that has assets in a form readily convertible into cash, and which have their own investment value irrespective of any current business use, a majority shareholding in such a company may be valued solely on a net assets basis, or on a "hybrid" basis (Chapter 7), and thereby reflect the respective importance of the assets on the one hand and the earnings from those assets on the other. If the investment assets can be separated from the business assets it will be necessary to include the value of the investment assets (or their income derivative) plus the capitalised earnings as two separate factors included as one total value. By business assets is meant those assets which are the source of or used for the purpose of earning, investment income or trading income, which income can be capitalised.

Alternatively, the value of the business assets may be very great yet produce a low yield in income terms, such as in the case of property investment companies. Here, the real value of the underlying assets would often be reflected in a very high capitalisation factor for the earnings.

Typically, these approaches will apply to property or investment companies and possibly also to companies owning intellectual property (patents, copyrights, licences etc) or possibly a ship-owning company; but it will be realised that the asset value will be taken only if demonstrably greater than the other possible bases. It may well be that the reason the earnings basis is low is a general decline in the particular industry or the economy generally, and that a corresponding problem could be found in disposing of the company's assets. For example, during a temporary decline in the shipping industry it might be found that perfectly good ships simply cannot be sold, and the discount that it would be necessary to apply to the current value to find a disposal value would be surprisingly, albeit factually, large. So, the earnings basis may still be appropriate after all when these factors are considered. Other relevant factors will be the quality of. the underlying assets, and the geographical and economic spread of the assets.

*Minority shareholders*

The valuation of a minority shareholding in such a company poses an interesting problem. A minority shareholding would usually be valued not on an assets basis, but on a dividend basis, that value possibly being influenced by the strength of the company's asset-backing by way of adjusting the discount for lack of marketability to reflect that strength and therefore the attraction of the shareholding in the hypothetical market. But if the company is in liquidation or about to go into liquidation a minority shareholding will be valued on an asset basis. The asset basis may also be appropriate for a minority shareholding where there is a clear asset-strip opportunity.

In *M'Connels Trustees*, Lord Fleming said "A purchaser of a small lot of shares would naturally have assumed that purchasers of the remaining shares would wish to make the most they could out of their shares and would concur with him in taking the necessary steps to have the assets of the company realised to the best advantage". But this view cannot have universal application: there must be many circumstances where the purchaser of shares in a company would maintain the company and keep the business intact even if no profits were being made, especially so where the purchaser would be involved in the day to day running of the business and rewarded by way of remuneration. Indeed, it should be understood that in the case of *M'Connel's Trustees*, Lord Fleming was considering purchasers buying shares *as an ordinary investment.*

The case of *Battle* v *IRC* provides useful guidance in valuing shares for the purposes of a minority sharehold-ing, where there is a single underlying asset. In that case, the company's only asset was a holding in British Gas stock. It was held that a substantial discount (15%) from the asset value of the share would be correct because amongst other things, the shareholder (1) could have acquired such stock personally without incurring a transfer stamp duty on the shares and (2) he could sell a personal holding of such stock without any restriction, whereas a disposal of the company shares was subject to restrictions set out in the company's Articles of Association. This sort of company must be distinguished from a company with an investment or property portfolio, where there may be earnings and dividends.

Where investment assets are owned in addition to assets used for business purposes, they would be valued independently of the business assets.

See also Combination Basis at 7.4.

## 6.6 Balance sheet values

In every case of share valuation, the net asset value of the company must be investigated to determine whether it is relevant to the valuation. The company's balance sheet will show the historic cost or revaluation of such assets and such values should be used as a starting point to identify the true market value at the required date. Even if the net asset value is not expected to be used in the calculation of the share value, it may nevertheless be a useful cross-check for the valuation basis that has been adopted and, as mentioned above, the net asset value may well influence the discount for non-marketability (see 2.16). If an asset value is grossly at variance from the proposed valuation obviously it would be necessary to investigate the reasons for this. For example, if the net asset value is vastly in excess of the capitalised earnings, the valuer may have discovered something about the company that the directors or owners did not know or refused to accept. Alternatively, it may simply show that the valuer has undercapitalised the earnings.

It is the *net* asset value that provides the true asset-backing figure. Liabilities must be taken into account, for if the company's assets are to be liquidated, creditors must be paid off. Such matters are dealt with below. The market value of each asset and liability must be considered independently but any inter-dependence or relationship should be brought into account as appropriate. If, for example, a loan is secured on a specific asset, the value of the asset in excess of the outstanding loan debt will be a surplus belonging to the company, unless the reality is that, on a break-up, after costs of sale etc, it would be cheaper to give the asset to the creditor in full and final settlement. As another example of asset inter-dependence a set of antique boardroom furniture will be of greater value than the sum of the individual knock-down prices of each item. In valuing the assets of a company which is a *going concern* it would not be correct to look at the break-up basis unless there is a clear indication that the asset should be disposed of and not replaced.

## 6.7 Valuing assets

The normal requirement is that open market value is to be taken. The principles of such open market price are discussed in Chapter 2. The rest of this Chapter considers special points to keep in mind in respect of specific assets.

## 6.8 Land and buildings

Normally, existing or current use value would be taken (ie the value of the land on the basis of the use to which the land is put at the date for valuation). But additionally a value should be given for any actual development permission, although great caution should be exercised over putting "hope" value on the land. Alternative use value of the land may also be considered, but that value would only displace the existing use value if the land is not required for the company's business, or if the alternative use value is demonstrably greater than the value of the company's business — which is not entirely unusual.

If valuing the land on an alternative use basis the cost of site clearance, levelling, infilling etc, should be taken into account, and regard should be had to any plant and/or machinery or structure on the land for, in such a case, they could not be valued on a current use basis unless the valuation of both land and buildings together on a current use basis is greater than the alternative use basis. It may be necessary to adopt a break-up basis for the plant etc, in which case the costs of dismantling, removing and restoring would have to be taken into account.

Existing tenancies and sub-tenancies, licences to occupy and covenants must also be brought into account.

Civil engineering works, plant and industrial structures will require specialist valuation. Because no ready market will exist for, say, an oil refinery, it would be necessary to take the current depreciated replacement cost in the case of a continuing business and to discount that value to reflect the remaining efficient and productive life of the asset as against the expected life of a new asset. This exercise would take into account factors such as possible technological and economic obsolescence of the asset; and technical and production specifications of the existing and new replacement assets would be compared because it may prove necessary to adapt or replace such assets in order to meet projected sales figures or merely to maintain current production levels.

If the company is being liquidated or the trade ceasing the assets would be valued on a break-up basis, special care being taken to separate those assets having intrinsic value and those with only scrap value, and the costs of dismantling and transportation will be relevant. Also, if there is any obligation under a lease or local or national law to leave the site in any particular state, ie completely levelled or landscaped etc, the cost of doing this should be taken into account.

## 6.9 Plant and machinery and structures

The value of land and buildings will usually be determined by a chartered surveyor who may also be skilled in valuing plant and machinery, especially where it forms part of a building or structure. Examples include transformer sub-stations, generating plant, escalators and lifting gear rails, boilers, air conditioning plant, sprinkler systems and other items forming an integral part of the structure of the building or other edifice. This would not normally include plant or machinery which is installed wholly or primarily in connection with industrial or commercial processes and other "loose" plant and machinery. For example, although the rails and gantry for an overhead crane may be included in the valuation of the building of which the rails or gantry form part, the crane itself would be valued as a separate and distinct asset. Structures which have been installed or erected in or on buildings or land for the provision of the services attaching thereto and *not forming part of any particular industrial or commercial process* would normally be included in the value of the building or land. Examples are boiler houses, chimneys, stagings, permanent partitioning and internal buildings, railways and bridges, fences, roads and hardstandings.

## 6.10 RICS open market price

In the Royal Institute of Chartered Surveyors *Guidance Notes on the Valuation of Assets* (2nd edition), the definition of open market value is the best price at which an interest in a property might reasonably be expected to be sold by private treaty at the date of valuation assuming:

    (i)  a willing seller;

    (ii)  a reasonable period within which to negotiate the sale taking into account the nature of the property and the state of the market;

    (iii)  values will remain static throughout the period;

    (iv)  the property will be freely exposed to the market;

    (v)  no account is to be taken of an additional bid by a special purchaser.

Of course, these guidelines will provide a value, but not necessarily the appropriate value for tax purposes. For example, the special purchaser cannot be dismissed for the purposes of a valuation for tax purposes, and the RICS value must be adjusted, if appropriate, to reflect the presence of such a purchaser; see 2.11.

RICS also defines the forced sale concept — this is the open market value as above except that the vendor has imposed a time limit for completion which cannot be regarded as a "reasonable period" as required in (ii) above.

## 6.11 Partial construction or development

In some cases property may be in the course of construction or may be held as trading stock. Specialised properties will be valued according to the existing stage of construction on a depreciated replacement cost basis, particularly having regard to whether the proposed current use would be the same after the share transfer. For example, it may be necessary to discount the proposed current use and substitute an alternative use basis, eg because the particular business for which the building is being constructed is to cease: in such a case the cost of removing or adapting the partially completed building must be brought into account. A non-specialist property is valued at the open market value of the land for the proposed use plus the cost of the development to the date of valuation. Alternatively the estimated current use value of the finished building, less the costs of completion, may be used.

## 6.12 Land as trading stock

Properties held as trading stock, if purchased and resold in the same unaltered condition, could be valued at the lower of cost or current market value, or where this cannot be ascertained, at original cost plus the cost of any development. See below for partially completed investment property. On liquidation market value would be the proper measure of value if ascertainable.

## 6.13 Rental properties

In the case of let properties it is necessary to look first at the current lease and secondly, if appropriate, at the rent potential after the expiry of the lease. First, the rent for the remaining period of the unexpired lease payable under the terms and conditions of the lease is capitalised, having regard to the basis and dates of rent reviews. Secondly the anticipated future open market value rental income based on normal lease terms would be capitalised and then discounted to a present day value.

Outgoings such as rates and water rates, agent and management fees and rents payable to a superior land-lord must also be taken into the equation. So too should any liability that can be identified and quantified with a reasonable degree of certainty. A repair and refurbish-ment clause, or a covenant to improve, putting the responsibility on the shoulders of the lessor, for example, would be an important future liability that should be provided for out of rents. There may already be a fund in existence out of which the future liability will be met, and if this is the case no further provision would need to be made unless the fund is calculated to meet the future liability by taking a contribution from future rents. Usually, of course, the lease will be a full repairing and insuring lease making the lessee responsible for the rates, repairs, maintenance, management and insurance (either directly or by way of service charge).

Other factors that can affect the value of property, whether or not rented, are:

- option to purchase, or for a new lease;
- planning applications or decisions (consents or refusals);
- zoning or compulsory purchase possibilities;
- mortgages and charges;
- easements.

Properties for letting which are in the course of being constructed will be valued according to the capitalised value of the expected rents when completed, less the estimated cost of completing the construction or development. If completion of construction or develop-ment is some way off it may not be appropriate to value in this way but rather to take the current land value plus the costs of the construction or development to date. Large developments of houses or flats for resale will probably be treated as trading stock (see above).

## 6.14 Negative value

Properties which constitute a liability to a company will

have a negative value. These normally are leasehold properties where the rent exceeds market value or where the lessee is bound by onerous covenants. As mentioned above, if there is responsibility to reinstate land to its former character at the end of some special use permitted by a local authority, the costs of so doing may be greater than the expected market value of the land at that time.

A negative cash flow arising from widely diverse properties would be capitalised at the (negative) value required out of which the negative cash flow can be met over a given period.

## 6.15 Premises and goodwill

For certain specialist commercial premises the building will itself form part of or include some or all of the goodwill of the business in which it is used. Examples are hotels, restaurants, cinemas, and skating rinks. In such cases the value of the "whole", ie the business, will, in the case of a going concern, be greater than the alternative use value of the "part", ie the premises in which the business is carried on. The premises themselves would only be valued independently of the goodwill on a break-up basis, when presumably there would be no "goodwill" to value, and in this case the premises would be valued on an alternative use basis or simply land value, possibly with costs of demolition brought into account — but take note of the effect of a "special purchaser" in the market — see 2.11 and 6.19.

## 6.16 Wasting assets (other than leaseholds)

Fixed assets which, when consumed, cannot be renewed in the existing location will be valued on the net current replacement cost basis as explained above. This includes mineral-bearing land, waste tips etc. The factors that will be relevant to this valuation are:

- volume of remaining reserves and royalty value;
- quality of remaining reserves;

- cost (revenue and capital) of recovering the remaining reserves;
- supply, demand and transportation factors;
- tenure, costs of concessions, royalty payments;
- alternative use value after exhaustion;
- alternative use value of land not yet required for working;
- costs of exploration, testing etc; incurred or yet to be incurred.

Non-mineral-bearing land such as rubbish tips will be valued similarly but by reference to filling-up rather than emptying. It may also be necessary to consider the value of a hole for such a purpose (planning permissions allowing) after minerals have been extracted by quarrying etc.

## 6.17 Investments

Shares held in a subsidiary unquoted company will need to be valued according to the appropriate share valuation basis — not necessarily using the same valuation basis as that adopted for the valuation of the parent company shares; as with all share valuations, the valuation basis depends upon the full circumstances and the size of the holding.

Shares held in quoted companies would be valued by reference to their quoted price on the day.

For the purposes of capital gains tax, corporation tax on chargeable gains and capital transfer tax/inheritance tax, the value of quoted shares and securities is determined as follows:

"The market value of shares or securities listed in The Stock Exchange Daily Official List shall, except where in consequence of special circumstances prices quoted in that List are by themselves not a proper measure of market value, be as follows:-

(a) the lower of the two prices shown in the quotations for the shares or securities in The Stock Exchange Daily Official list on the relevant date plus one-quarter of the difference between those two figures, or

(b) halfway between the highest and lowest prices at which bargains, other than bargains done at special prices, were recorded in the shares or securities for the relevant date,

choosing the amount under paragraph (a) if less than that under paragraph (b), or if no such bargains were recorded for the relevant date, and choosing the amount under paragraph (b) if less than that under paragraph (a):

Provided that —

(i) this subsection shall not apply to shares or securities for which The Stock Exchange provides a more active market elsewhere than on the London trading floor, and

(ii) if the London trading floor is closed on the relevant date the market value shall be ascertained by reference to the latest previous date or earliest subsequent date on which it is open, whichever affords the lower market value."

The foregoing "quarter-up" or "halfway" rules are specified in Capital Gains Tax Act 1979 s.150; and are adopted for capital transfer tax/inheritance tax purposes. The Stock Exchange Daily Official List records all the day's bargains up to 2.15pm. Bargains after that time are recorded in the next day's list and are flagged.

The quoted price will include allowance for accrued dividends or interest, which will belong to the owner as at a specified date after the date the dividend is declared. A sale before that date will take the expected dividend with the shares; a sale after that date will exclude the recent dividend. Once that date has passed therefore the List shows the share price as being "xd" (ie ex-dividend or without any right to the latest declared dividend).

If no quotation is available for the day of valuation (for example, because the Stock Exchange is closed) the last quoted price or the next following may be taken.

For foreign shares, the UK quoted price will normally be accepted by the SVD unless there is a dual register in which case the quotations on the local exchange will be taken — applying the "quarter-up" or "halfway" basis.

Where, exceptionally, the quoted price is not a proper measure of the market value, it cannot be taken for tax valuation purposes. For example, there may have been no bargains done for some considerable time or the shares are suspended for some reason. In such a case it would obviously be necessary to consider all the circumstances and information available concerning the shares.

## 6.18 Cash

A substantial amount of cash shown on the balance sheet indicates one of three things: first, a temporary reservoir of unallocated cash is held; secondly, a necessary cash reserve is maintained because the business requires ready cash; or thirdly, a surplus of reserves is held in cash form. It may be possible to confirm which of these is the case by comparing balance sheets of earlier years and satisfying oneself that there has been no inherent change in the conduct of the business or in its activities.

In the case of the third possibility, it may be argued that the cash represents undistributed reserves which are having no impact on the business itself or on the income and growth generating factors, in which case the cash and interest thereon should be regarded as an asset to one side of the business assets and therefore to be brought separately into account in the valuation. Alternatively or additionally, such a reserve may have a marked effect on a dividend basis unless the cash could be shown to be retained necessarily for a future business development purpose.

## 6.19 Goodwill

In simplistic terms goodwill is an intangible appendage to a business or to a business asset; it cannot exist in isolation. Goodwill, in the valuation of a business in its entirety, will be that part of the total value that exceeds the value of the net tangible assets. In order for there to be such an excess, the expected annual maintainable profits of the business must be greater than a reasonable financial return from the investment in those net tangible assets.

When valuing a business on a break-up basis, where the business is to cease altogether, goodwill will not exist in respect of the business as a whole because it is implicit in goodwill that a profit-earning potential exists, yet there may be goodwill attaching to individual assets or groups of assets. A case in point might be a hotel group. Some hotels in the group may be profitable, some not so. On a break-up basis, each hotel will be segregated and looked at in isolation or, possibly, in viable groups depending on size.

"Goodwill" is:

> "the benefit and advantage of the good name, reputation, and connection of a business. It is the attractive force which brings in custom. It is the one thing which distinguishes an old established from a new business at its first start. The goodwill of a business must emanate from a particular centre or source. However widely extended or diffused its influence may be, goodwill is worth nothing unless it has power of attraction sufficient to bring customers to the source from which it emanates. Goodwill is composed of a variety of elements. It differs in its composition in different trades and in different businesses in the same trade. ... The goodwill of a business is one whole ...

> "... If there is one attribute common to all cases of goodwill, it is the attribute of locality. For goodwill has no independent existence. It cannot subsist by itself. It must be attached to a business. Destroy the business and the goodwill perishes with it, though the elements remain which may perhaps be gathered up and revived again."

Having said all this, Lord MacNaughten, in the stamp duty case *IRC* v *Muller & Co's Margarine Ltd*, admitted that in his terms it may be difficult to localise goodwill where the reputation of a business is very widely spread, or where it is the article produced rather than the producer of the article that has won popular favour.

In the same case Lord Brampton distinguished two forms of goodwill. The first is goodwill together with the premises in which the trade is then carried on, whereby the value of the premises is enhanced. In this case the trade and the premises are inseparable so long as the trade is carried on there; it is, acccording to Lord Brampton, immaterial whether the business has been built up by reason of the personal good qualities of the outgoer, the goodness of his wares or merchandise, the good situation of the premises, or the absence of competition; the business and custom in fact have been attracted to the premises, and when the incomer takes possession he takes all the chances offered and conveyed to him by the purchase, of standing, so far as the business is concerned, in the shoes of the outgoer, and he must rely upon his own good qualities and aptitude of his undertaking to continue the prosperity of the business and thereby profit by his bargain.

The second is goodwill utterly unconnected with the premises in which it is carried on, and which is merely the advantage of the recommendation of the vendor to his connections and customers and his covenant to allow the vendee to use his trade name and to abstain from competition with him.

It is not at all easy to define goodwill, but more often than not in share valuations, it is not necessary to take great pains to identify it. In an asset valuation, however, one is engaged in breaking down the valuable constituent parts of the company. If there are assets that can realise cash and are replaceable without changing the nature or the intrinsic value of the business, then those can be regarded as separate from the goodwill. However, if an asset is part of the very nature of the business and income can be said to emanate from it, it would be wrong to try to separate it from the goodwill of the business as a whole, unless the company has been continuously unprofitable and is being valued on a break-up basis. In that case it is likely that there is no goodwill for the business as a whole, although, as was illustrated above, goodwill can attach to independent assets.

In the case of intellectual property, such as patents, copyrights, trade-marks, licences, know-how, design registration (all intangible assets because they are "rights" and as such have no physical presence in themselves) it would be wrong to regard such property as separate from goodwill because they will be the very source of the earnings of the business. In the event of a break-up basis valuation, each such asset would be considered independently and valued on the basis of the income that could be expected to be earned from its continued exploitation having regard to its expected exploitable life. Rather like property, the valuation of intellectual property is a highly specialised area requiring specialist valuation.

Assets that would need replacing regularly, even if over a period of years, are unlikely to form part of the nature of the business because they are replaceable and replaced. An ice-cream van, on the other hand, may be the actual source of income — the fixed premises — and the asset would last as long as the income earning potential of the business. Without the van, all the income would "melt" away. In this case, the value of the vehicle and of the income earning potential are one. A similar principle applies, for example, to a sweet shop. It is conceivable however, that the value of the "goodwill" may be less than the alternative use value of the sweetshop, and in such a case clearly the value of the property would displace that of the goodwill. Again, considering the ice-cream van, there may additionally be some value in "know-how" — how to produce a proper ice-cream cornet, or the most profitable route for the van to take, and the most profitable time of day to visit key sales areas. The value of this information is probably something less than the earnings that would theoretically be lost while discovering the know-how on a trial and error basis. This value too would form part of the goodwill.

In some businesses, particularly service industries, the goodwill is very personal to an individual and the business would cease if that individual died or retired. But there are clearly many cases where the goodwill will continue beyond an individual's death or retirement, even where the goodwill originally derived from the individual.

## 6.20 Valuation of goodwill

Broadly speaking, the value of goodwill is the difference between the capitalised value of the earnings and the value of net tangible assets. In the case of *Findlay's Trustees* v *IRC*, a case concerning the value of a newspaper business, it was common ground that for the purposes of ascertaining a business's net profits, those profits should be before tax and interest on debentures, and that the agreed profit figure — that which the purchaser could reasonably expect to earn from the business — should be multiplied by 8 to give the total value of the business and from that figure the value of net tangible assets is removed to give the goodwill value. But the parties disagreed on how to arrive at the appropriate profit figure. One party took the average of the last three years and the other party took the final year's profits.

Lord Fleming said:

> "... when one is seeking to ascertain the profits which will probably be earned by a business in the future, it is quite usual to do so by taking an average of the profits actually earned for the three preceding years. This probably operates quite equitably when one is dealing with a well established business, which has normal ups and downs, but has no violent fluctuations in either direction. But if there is a definite trend upwards or downwards, it may be different."

In this particular case it was found that the last year in question showed a heavily reduced profit and Fleming said in respect of it:

> "... it is impossible to avoid coming to the conclusion that the outlook in 1930 could not be regarded as favourable for the newspaper industry ... A prudent buyer would, I think, proceed upon the view that the business would not recover from the serious setback which it had sustained in 1930 for some years."

Lord Fleming eventually settled for a profit figure (£135,000) that was almost exactly halfway between the three year average (£147,510) and the final year (£124,721). What he was seeking to achieve was to strike a profit that could reasonably be expected to be maintained by the business without the interference of any special outside influence or person — thus any "personal" goodwill element would be excluded unless the right to exploit that personal goodwill was somehow retained in the business. At the same time it would be necessary to consider whether the business might be "disturbed" by the actions of the vendor after the disposal, and to adjust the profits for any expected competition that might follow the sale. Normally, a shopkeeper (as many other types of entrepreneur) would be prevented from exercising a similar trade or business within a radius of, say, five or thirty miles of the location of the business being sold, or perhaps some other restrictive covenant would apply (provided it is not an oppressive or unenforceable restriction) and this may be brought into the formula.

As has been shown above, once a maintainable profit is determined, the profit must be capitalised by multiplying it by a factor appropriate to the type of business and economic activity. Deciding what that factor should be is difficult indeed, and better considered on the basis of the factors in Chapter 5.

Once the capitalised value for the whole business has been determined, the value of net assets is removed (but not of any assets which are necessarily bound into the goodwill, such as the sweetshop or hotel previously discussed). What is left is the value of the goodwill of the business. This is the total capitalisation method.

An alternative method is to calculate the annual yield that arises — or should arise — from the tangible assets used in the business, deduct that from the annual maintainable profits and then multiply the difference by a capitalisation factor. This method is known as the super profits method.

These two methods are common in valuing substantial

businesses. Theoretically they should both give the same result and the value determined under one of the methods should be capable of being put into the formula for the other to give an acceptable yield under that formula. If that is not the case, then, in theory at least, the yields and/or capitalisation factors used in one or other, or both, of the methods must be suspect.

Under the *total capitalisation* method, the maintainable profits are multiplied by a capitalisation factor which is determined by the yield expected from the investment in the business as a whole.

Under the *super profits* method, two yields are required: the first, a lower yield, from the investment in the net tangible assets; and the second, a higher yield, from the investment in the pure goodwill. The yields, one for tangible assets and one for goodwill, at best may be debatable and arbitrary.

An example will help to show the two different methods:

Suppose a business has proven maintainable profits of £100,000 and tangible assets valued at £400,000. What value should be placed on the goodwill of the business?

Looking first at the *super profits* method, the yield required from the investment in the tangible assets must be estimated, remembering the alternative investments available, such as gilts or bank deposits or the money market. It would normally be the case that the yield expected from tangible assets would be less than that expected from pure goodwill.

For the purposes of this example, let us suppose a yield of 12% is required:

| | | |
|---|---|---|
| Yield required from fixed assets — say 12% | £48,000 | 400,000 |
| Super-profit £100,000 − £48,000 = | £52,000 | |
| Three year purchase of goodwill @ £52,000 | | 156,000 |
| Total value | | £556,000 |

The other variable factor is the three year purchase of goodwill which gives a yield of 33 1/3rd.

The total capitalisation method will agree with the super profits method *if the capitalisation factor for the business as a whole* will give £556,000 when applied to maintainable profits. One way to determine the value of goodwill is to calculate the values under both methods and compare values falling within a common value range. It is helpful in the calculations only to use whole number capitalisation factors and to allow a margin for error of +/− 1. This gives the "range". If the two methods give comparable values within this range it might be reasonable to take the simple average of those two values.

Suppose, for example, that we consider the capitalisation factor for this sort of business as a whole in the current economic climate to be 5 (equivalent to an annual yield of 20%).

| | VALUE RANGE | | |
| --- | --- | --- | --- |
| | A | B | C |
| *Total capitalisation method* | (5−1) | 5 | (5+1) |
| Total value of business (x £100,000) | 400,000 | 500,000 | 600,000 |
| Less: tangible assets | 400,000 | 400,000 | 400,000 |
| Value of goodwill | NIL | 100,000 | 200,000 |
| *Super-profits method* | (3−1) | 3 | (3+1) |
| Purchase of goodwill (x £52,000) | 104,000 | 156,000 | 208,000 |
| Add: Tangible assets | 400,000 | 400,000 | 400,000 |
| Total value of the business | 504,000 | 556,000 | 608,000 |

The value range for the total value of the business under the total capitalisation method is £400,000 >£600,000.

The value range for the super-profits method is £504,000 >£608,000.

The total capitalisation value of the business (B) is £500,000. It will be seen that this is outside the value range for the super profits methods — it is lower than £504,000. Therefore, £504,000 should be taken as the minimum value.

The super profits value of the business is £556,000. This is within the value range for the total capitalisation method (£400,000 >£600,000) and we may therefore regard *£556,000* as the maximum value (had it been outside that value range, at say £606,000 the maximum value would have been limited to £600,000).

The average of these values (£504,000 and £556,000) is *£530,000*. As the assets are valued at £400,000, the value of the goodwill is £530,000 − £400,000 = *£130,000*.

Relating this to the first assumptions:

- On the basis of maintainable profits of £100,000 and a 12% yield from fixed assets, the resultant yield of £52,000 out of the goodwill value of £130,000 represents a 2.5 years purchase, or a yield of 40%. If this is considered to be too high, is the yield from the fixed assets too low?

- On the basis of maintainable profits of £100,000 the value of the business at £530,000 gives a capitalisation factor of 5.3, equivalent to an annual yield of 18.9%.

This example is merely a way of averaging out guesses within an arbitrary compass. Yet it may help to contain the inexactitude so often encountered in goodwill valuation.


## 6.21 Negative goodwill

A low level of profitability may give rise to a negative goodwill or to "super losses". This occurs when more money may be realised from disposing of the assets on a break up basis. The cessation of trading may itself create further losses through crystallising a liability, for example, to make redundancy payments.

In the smaller, unincorporated "one-man" type of business, less importance will be placed on establishing a yield from the tangible assets employed and it is even likely that no deduction will be made from net profits for remuneration to the owner. This resultant over-blown profit will be multiplied by a factor representing a number of years' purchase, or alternatively, goodwill may be derived from turnover.

In these cases Shares Valuation Division will seek to value the business by reference to actual sales of similar businesses, and a good guide would be to obtain particulars of sales of businesses from the specialist press such as *Dalton's Weekly* or *Exchange and Mart*. More often than not, such businesses include a premises and, as mentioned earlier, the value of the premises will effectively incorporate the value of the goodwill. In the case of leasehold property the Shares Valuation Division will regard a 21 year lease as secure as a freehold and they will therefore resist a discount on leaseholds of that duration or longer.

A number of cases (*Nielsen* v *London Borough of Camden*; *Perezic* v *Bristol Corporation*, and *Zarraga* v *Newcastle upon Tyne Corporation*) has shown that usually no remuneration should be deducted in determining profits for the purpose of valuing goodwill in the case of one-man or husband and wife businesses. But in *R C Handley Ltd* v *London Borough of Greenwich* a nominal deduction for management remuneration and 10% interest on capital were allowed from profits of £14,000 a year. This principle was extended to directors' remuneration in *Lewis's Executors and Palladium Cinema (Brighton) Ltd* v *Brighton Corporation* where the company's profits were generated by one man. But all these cases were compensation claims against local authorities for loss of goodwill, and although goodwill may form part of a company's assets, it is difficult to conceive of shares having a value which is based on no cost of earning the company's profits — ie the cost of labour and management.

As mentioned earlier, in many businesses — and this includes many small "one-man" or family companies — the goodwill is attached to an individual and dies with him. The Shares Valuation Division may accept this if the company is to be liquidated and no-one is to take over the business.

# Chapter 7

# The hybrid basis and the combination basis

## 7.1 The alternative bases

There are occasions when a single valuation basis will not be appropriate, for example, because a shareholder has different expectations from his shares depending upon the view that is taken about the prospects for, say, increased earnings or dividends or the realisation of asset value.

In these cases it may be appropriate to take into account all the valuation bases (assets, earnings and dividends and yields) and apply them separately to different assets, or to weight them according to their respective importance. Some authorities on the subject also bring into account a weighting for prior sales if there have been any. However, in the author's view a prior sale should be used only as a means of checking a current value and should not be used to distort values calculated under the standard valuation bases.

This Chapter is concerned with two variants on the standard valuation bases; the hybrid basis and the combination basis.

The *hybrid basis* is where two or more bases are used in tandem, a full valuation under each base being under-taken but only a percentage of each value being used according to the relative importance of each to the total value. Thus, supposing 30% of Company A's shares are valued as follows: asset valuation £3 per share; earnings valuation £4 per share; dividends £1 per share, and it is thought appropriate to give the following weights to each respectively: 60%; 30%; 10%, the value would become (60% x £3) + (30% x £4) + (10% x £1) = *£3.10* per share (before any discount for lack of marketability).

A hybrid basis cannot apply if there are no earnings and no future earnings in prospect. In that case there can be no future dividend stream in prospect either and value can be found on an assets basis only.

If there are no assets or, more likely, only nominal assets and no prospects for future dividends, only an earnings basis can identify value in the shares; with the result that minority shareholders will probably have nil value shares.

It is unlikely that the hybrid method of valuation can be relevant to a going concern trading company for shareholdings outside the range of 20% to 74%. Below that range the dividend basis cannot be ousted; above it the earnings basis must surely be supreme.

For investment companies however the range may be from 0% to 74% because the value of solid asset backing may percolate through to the smallest of shareholdings. Above the range, the asset basis will probably be appropriate unless capitalised earnings exceed the asset value, in which case the earnings basis will apply.

Within these ranges of shareholding the hybrid basis may be used and the problem is to identify when to use it and to choose the appropriate percentage of each valuation basis.

## 7.2 When to choose the hybrid basis

The hybrid basis can be appropriate in many cases and the valuer should consider using it when he feels, having looked at all the underlying facts relating to the shareholding, the company, its business, assets and future, that there is more (or less) to the value of the shares in the context of the size and influence of the shareholding and the circumstances of the valuation than a straight application of one basis would give. For example, a small minority shareholding would normally be valued on a dividends basis. However, if the earnings of the company are extremely high and the dividends have been kept very low or are non-existent because earnings are retained for business purposes, and if the reserves are accumulating and the business is progressing well, clearly there is an argument that the benefit of holding the shares may be found in the accumulating earnings which will enure for the future benefit of the shareholder, and therefore some weighting should be given both to the earnings basis, from which value is evident, and to the asset basis in respect of accumulated but unrequired cash.

Where the company has under-utilised assets, or the value of the assets is greater than the capitalised value of the earnings they are producing, some weighting should be attached to an asset valuation. Clearly, where assets are minimal and value stems from the utilisation of labour the weighting should be in favour of earnings rather than assets, and so on. As has already been mentioned, particular attention should be paid to investment companies whose asset value may well exceed capitalised earnings and dividends.

## 7.3 Weighting

Attempting to approach this in some scientific fashion it is necessary to categorise the possible different shareholding environments within the hybrid valuation range:

1. the shareholding has control (ie 51% to 74%);
2. the shareholding has effective control because it is the largest single shareholding and exceeds 25% (ie 26%–50%);
3. no shares have effective control (ie 26%–50%);
4. no shares have effective control (ie up to 25%);
5. other shareholdings have control (ie up to 49%).

The following are merely broad suggestions for weightings, which will be influenced by the facts of each case:

| Shareholding Environment | Weighting % (investment company in parentheses) | | |
|---|---|---|---|
| | Asset | Earnings | Dividend |
| 1. Control (51% to 74%) | 20 (50) | 75 (50) | 5 (−) |
| 2. Effective control (26% to 50%) | 20 (40) | 65 (20) | 15 (40) |
| 3. No controlling interest (26%-50%) | 10 (30) | 40 (20) | 50 (50) |
| 4. No controlling interest (up to 25%) | 10 (20) | 25 (10) | 65 (70) |
| 5. Control elsewhere (up to 49%) | 5 (20) | 20 (5) | 75 (75) |

## 7.4 The combination basis

The combination basis is simply where, notwithstanding that an ordinary share in a company does not entitle the shareholder to ownership of individual assets, certain of the assets and business that the company owns need to be independently valued. In this case the total share valuation is the combined value as independently determined.

*Separate investment assets* are assets which can be separated from the company's business assets and which can stand alone as investments in their own right. For a majority shareholder either the value of those assets, or the capitalised value of the income derived from them, would be added to the capitalised value of the business earnings. A minority shareholding would be valued on the normal dividend basis, but to reflect the additional asset backing, extra value should be added even if there is little chance of actually realising the value directly from the asset. The combination method would achieve this by separate evaluation of the individual assets, identifying their probable individual worth to the particular shareholder, and aggregating the values. Alternatively, this extra value may be added by reducing the discount for lack of marketability to reflect the extra attraction of the shareholding in the hypothetical market; or a percentage of the minority shareholding value might be attributed to the value of the company on an assets basis, under the hybrid basis, explained above; or the income (if any) could be capitalised with the earnings from the company's business and a higher PER attributed to reflect the strong asset-backing.

139

## *Example:*

Suppose the asset market-values of a company were:

Non business assets      £100,000 (non income producing)
Business assets        £ 75,000 (regularly yielding 20% post tax)

A dividend policy has been established and 30% of profits are regularly paid out. A minority shareholding of 5% is to be valued. The required yield is 12% (ie capitalise gross dividends of 100/12).

*Dividend basis valuation*

| | | | |
|---|---|---|---|
| 1. | Earnings – £75,000 @ 20% yield | = | £15,000 |
| 2. | Dividends – £15,000 @ 30% paid | = | £ 4,500 |
| 3. | Gross dividends – £4,500 @ 10/7 (ACT) | = | £ 6,500 |
| 4. | Capitalised value – £6,500 @ 12% grossed | = | £54,000 |
| 5. | Discount for lack of marketability, say (40%) leaving – £54,000 @ 60% | = | £32,400 |
| 6. | 5% shareholding – £32,400 @ 5/100 | = | £ 1,620 |

But, can this be the final valuation when there are additional assets of £100,000 available? 5% of that value would be £5,000, but there is no likelihood of the 5% shareholder actually receiving that value until the company realises the cash and either distributes it as a dividend or upon liquidation. The chances of that happening must be quantified if at all possible because it is a material factor to the current value.

It is assumed that there is less than 10% chance of that money being realised within the next five years, but a good chance of it being realised thereafter.

It can also be assumed that there will be someone in the hypothetical open market who is prepared to wait some considerable time before taking the fruits of his investment. He may not be prepared to wait forever. On the other hand, he might expect to find another such purchaser at some future time who is likewise prepared to wait to recover his investment.

These long-term investors will need to be satisfied that the investment is sound and secure and that there will be an adequate return for their patience to compensate them for the loss of income and opportunity that would have been available if the investment had been placed elsewhere. The risk involved must be quantified. It might rule out making the investment or it might mean that a higher return is required.

We may assume that a yield on a secure asset that is likely to be realised for cash between five to ten years time — say, seven years as an acceptable working figure — is 11%. There is some uncertainty about whether the asset will be realised for cash for the benefit of shareholders; there is also uncertainty that the asset will maintain a growth in value that will equal or exceed inflation; the asset itself may carry intrinsic depreciatory factors or be subject to possible fluctuations in value; it might be found in time that the asset cannot or will not be realised within the expected time scale. Because of that uncertainty a higher return than the 11% associated with a secure and certain investment will be required. Assuming that the asset is sound enough, nevertheless the risks are there and cannot be denied. It will also be recalled (see 3.1) that no shareholder has a right to any specific portion of the company's property. He cannot expect to force the company to sell the asset and distribute the proceeds unless he has voting control or perhaps in a case of oppression of minority interests.

A discount of 50% from the present day value of the asset is a sensible, commercial discount from which to start. This may of course vary according to the precise description and circumstances of the asset, but where such a long term delay before possible realisation is concerned 50% is a reasonable, one might say modest, rate. Because the proceeds from the realisation of the asset would still be locked into the company and are a constituent part of the value

# The hybrid basis and the combination basis

of the company's shares, the potential future realised value would also be reduced by the discount for lack of marketability — taken in this case as 40%. The present day value of £1 at the end of 7 years, discounted at 11% is approximately 48p. A valuation of the asset may then proceed:

*Asset based valuation of non-business asset*

| | | | |
|---|---|---|---|
| 1. Present day value − £100,000 @ 48p per £ | = | £48,000 | |
| 2. Discounted for uncertainty − £48,000 @ 50% leaves | | £24,000 | |
| 3. Discount for lack of marketability deducted (40%) − £24,000 @ 60% | = | £14,400 | |
| 4. 5% shareholding − £14,400 £5/100 | = | £ 720 | |

There are still some problems to consider however:

(a) First, the possibility that the asset is realised by the company and distributed to the shareholders as income. If there is a latent capital gains tax liability this should be reflected in the realisable value of the asset, ie under current law the charge would amount to 30% of the gain. If the asset was income-producing and there was no evidence to suppose that the asset would be sold then, perhaps, capital gains tax liability would not be a realistic reduction to take account of and the capitalised value of the income would be taken, but in other circumstances where a valuation is being based on the premise of a future realisation of value there is no reason to ignore the tax liability. Although additionally advance corporation tax would be payable on the distribution of the net receipt to the shareholder (currently 3/7ths of the dividend) making the immediate effective tax rate in the company 51% of the capital gain, the value of the distribution would be grossed-up to reflect the tax credit available, and therefore the ACT/tax credit effect would be neutral. The shareholder would effectively receive an amount equal to the value of the asset as reduced by the 30% tax charge on the gain, ie:

| | Distribution of proceeds £ | Distribution of gain only £ |
|---|---|---|
| Sale consideration | 100,000 | |
| Cost (say) | 20,000 | |
| Gain | 80,000 | 80,000 |
| Corporation tax on chargeable gain | 24,000 | 24,000 |
| Distributable amount (100 - 24) | 76,000 | 56,000 |
| Distribution | 53,200 | 39,200 |
| ACT/Tax credit | 22,800 | 16,800 |
| Value received by shareholders | 76,000 | 56,000 |

The valuation should not take account of the personal tax liability of the shareholder. Therefore the maximum tax liability that could be taken into account would be the effective tax charge in the company of 30%.

(b) Alternatively, the company might be liquidated and the asset paid up by way of liquidation distribution. In this case the effective tax rate in the company would still be 30%. The balance would be paid to the shareholder without any ACT/tax credit complications but would leave the recipient with his own potential capital gains tax liabilities.

Whichever way one looks at the picture, the actual value of the asset to the shareholder is likely to be less than its open market value if it is an asset, that, upon disposal, would attract capital gains tax.

(c) A third possibility is that the company would sell the asset (or borrow against its value) and then use the funds in the company and not distribute them to shareholders.

This alternative would have the effect of increasing the earnings, and thereby our dividend basis would be as follows (using the same investment criteria as adopted for the original dividend basis, above):

*Additional deemed dividend basis*

| | |
|---|---|
| 1. Capital base £100,000 less tax on gain | £76,000 |
| 2. Earnings – £76,000 @ 20% yield | £15,200 |
| 3. Dividends – £15,200 @ 30% paid | £4,560 |
| 4. Gross dividends – £4,560 @ 10/7 (ACT) | £6,500 |
| 5. Capitalised value – £6,500 @ 12% grossed | £54,000 |
| 6. Discount for uncertainty – £54,000 @ 50% | £27,000 |
| 7. Discount for lack of marketability deducted (40%) – £27,000 @ 60% | £16,200 |
| 8. 5% shareholders – £16,200 x 5/100 | £810 |

The £810 additional dividend basis value compares with the £720 additional asset basis value prior to any provision for tax on capital gains. In our example the effective tax rate on the whole asset value of £100,000 is 24% (£24,000 being the tax on the gain of £80,000). The additional asset basis value after a provision for capital gains tax would therefore become £720 less 24% = *£547*. The value may therefore be struck at between £547 and £810 – say, *£675*.

Thus the combined values of the 5% shareholding would be £1,600 + £675 = *£2,275*.

Another special case concerns business assets with value exceeding capitalised earnings value. Although there may not be assets that are additional to income-producing assets in a company there may well be income producing assets that have more value for their capital appreciation potential than for their income earning capacity.

## *Example:*

An investment company owns real property investments valued at say, £5m, and increasing in capital value at 18% per annum, returning 4% post tax in rents on an historic value basis, 70% of which is paid out in dividends. A 20% interest in this company on a dividend basis is likely to give a wholly erroneous value because there is an undeniable underlying value.

On a dividend basis, taking a required yield of 4.5% for average property investment company investments, and a discount for lack of marketability of 35%, the value might be as follows:

*Dividend basis valuation*

| | |
|---|---|
| 1. Earnings – £5m @ 4% yield | £200,000 |
| 2. Dividends – £200,000 @ 70% | £140,000 |
| 3. Gross dividends – £140,000 @ 10/7 (ACT) | £200,000 |

| | |
|---|---|
| 4. Capitalised value — £200,000 @ 100/4.5 | £4,500,000 |
| 5. Discount for lack of marketability say (35%)<br>   leaving — £4,500,000 @ 65% | £2,900,000 |
| 6. 20% shareholding — £2,900,000 x 20/100 | £580,000 |

The value of the 20% shareholding, on a break-up basis would be £1,000,000, less corporation tax on the gain made by the company, less costs of sale and liquidation — say, net £720,000; as a going concern the value would be £650,000 after discount for lack of marketability. An asset-valuation is inappropriate for a going concern because a 20% shareholder could not force a liquidation. But if the evidence is that the increase in the value of the asset backing is out-pacing the normal growth in property values plus inflation perhaps some compensatory value should be brought into account. Obviously, one might argue about the required yield taken for capitalisation purposes. At the date of writing, it probably would not be less than 4.5% (or possibly 6% in which case the differential in values would be even greater), but it will be appreciated that the yield is low for the very reason that the earnings emanate from land value — an additional value to reflect the growth in the company's asset value will be justified *only* if that growth is greater than that of the average property investment company plus the current rate of inflation. For the purposes of this example the excess growth is called the "growth differential".

It is assumed there is a 3% p.a. growth differential. So, present day value of one year's growth would be £5m @ 3% = £150,000. It is assumed that this growth is not actually contributing to any increase in earnings (but in the case of property investment companies, the value of rent revisions may be material to the valuation). We cannot bring in a revised dividend basis because there is no evidence (in this example) that the growth in capital value will be turned into additional earnings. Neither can we bring in any taxation provision because the assets are business assets producing income and the business is a going concern. One is therefore restricted to an assets valuation of the growth differential, thus:

*Asset based valuation of growth in capital value*

| | | |
|---|---|---|
| 1. Present day value of growth plus 1 year* | = | £150,000 |
| 2. Discounted for uncertainty — £150,000<br>   @ 50% | = | £75,000 |
| 3. Discount for lack of marketability say<br>   (35%) leaving — £75,000 @ 65% | = (say) | £50,000 |
| 4. 20% shareholding — £50,000 @ 20/100 | = | £10,000 |

Thus, the combined values of the shareholding would be £580,000 + £10,000 = £590,000.

\* See 4.3 for a discussion of dividend growth. The braver the valuer the longer the period of growth differential he would value.

Note in the foregoing examples, the discount for lack of marketability has been taken at maximum rates. In the case of good property asset backing, the discount could be as low as 10% and will, of course, depend upon the facts of each case. In any investment company share valuation the make-up of the investment portfolio (including geographical spread etc) is of paramount importance as also is the management ability. Specialist advice regarding individual valuation of investment must be sought because only intimate knowledge of the appropriate investment market will provide an accurate valuation.

The circumstances in the latter example particularly lend themselves to the hybrid valuation basis, which would attribute some of the valuation to the earnings basis and some to the assets basis. The example is considerably simplified, and it is likely that in reality the growth would be reflected in additional future earnings because it would increase borrowing power; this growth potential would therefore be reflected in the PER and certainly in a public quoted company comparison the quoted PER would reflect future growth expectations. But the example is useful to illustrate how to deal with other appreciating assets and with companies that cannot sensibly be compared with quoted companies.

# Chapter 8

# Taxation

## 8.1 Introduction

Share valuations are relevant in one way or another to all the direct taxes. Capital transfer tax/inheritance tax and capital gains tax lead the field; income tax is particularly relevant in the event of a transfer or issue of shares to an employee; stamp duty has not the same significance now that the making of a gift is exempt from duty, but it can otherwise still amount to a significant cost where values are high, and capital duty can be relevant in cases involving the issue of new share or securities. One of the most common requirements for a tax valuation is upon the making of a gift, but with stamp duty exemption and roll-over relief possibilities for capital gains tax, and the exempt bands and business asset relief for capital transfer tax and inheritance tax, together with a little forward planning, quite considerable amounts can be transferred without any immediate tax charge and often with a per-manent tax saving.

This book is not a tax planning book, however, and it would be inappropriate to present detailed advice here, especially as tax planning criteria change with each annual Budget and, often, between Budgets also.

The following sections of this Chapter deal with the current tax provisions relating to valuation.

## 8.2 Capital gains tax

*Bargains made otherwise than at arm's length*

When there is a disposal or acquisition of shares

145

otherwise than by way of a bargain made at arm's length, the market value of those shares is generally taken as the consideration for the shares. This is of particular relevance in cases of gifts, transfers into settlement or distributions from a company in respect of shares in the company. Market value will also be taken where the consideration (or some of it) cannot be valued (for example, a restrictive covenant or an option to acquire something in the future subject to the happening of some event outside anyone's control); or if the acquisition or disposal is in connection with an office or employment (Capital Gains Tax Act 1979 s.29A). As to approved share option schemes see also Finance Act 1984 s.38(3).

Note particularly that where a disposal and acquisition of shares is between "connected persons" the transaction will always be treated as being made "otherwise than by way of bargain made at arm's length" and the market value of those shares must be taken as the sole consideration for capital gains tax purposes (Capital Gains Tax Act 1979 s.62). The meaning of connected persons is set out in Capital Gains Tax Act 1979 s.63, but broadly includes spouses, brothers, sisters, ancestors and lineal descendants; partners and their relatives; settlors, trustees and companies whose shares are held by trustees; companies under common control; and, in relation to a company, any two or more persons acting together to secure or exercise control.

The market value rule in s.29A will not apply if there is *no corresponding disposal* of the asset and there is no consideration in money or money's worth, or the consideration is less than market value. This is an anti-avoidance rule to prevent an uplift in base value in certain situations.

Normally, the value of consideration given in kind will be its open market value, but in *Stanton* v *Drayton Commercial Investment Co Ltd*, where shares were offered in exchange for an asset and a sale contract specified the price of those shares, the shares were not required to be valued on a market value basis as was contended by the Inland Revenue. The agreed value of the shares had been honestly reached between the parties and the transaction was by way of bargain at arm's length.

A final point concerning connected party transactions is that s.62(5) requires that if the person making the disposal (or a person connected with him) has power to enforce a right or restriction in respect of the asset transferred, the market value of the asset is determined initially free of any such encumbrance and is then reduced by "the market value of the right or restriction or the amount by which its extinction would enhance the value of the asset to its owner (whichever is the less)". But such rights will be ignored for these purposes if, upon enforcement, the asset's value would be substantially impaired and no advantage would be brought to the disposer (but consider Capital Gains Tax Act, 1979 s.25 as to value shifting). In the case of incorporeal assets, rights of extinguishment are also ignored for this purpose.

Relief from Capital Gains Tax is available by hold-over of realisation of assets under Finance Act 1979 s.79. This effective postponement of the tax charge means that a valuation will not be needed for Capital Gains Tax or stamp duty purposes.

## Trust distribution

When a person becomes absolutely entitled to settled property as against the trustee, the assets forming part of that property are deemed to be disposed of by the trustee and immediately re-acquired by him as trustee for a consideration equal to the market value (Capital Gains Tax Act 1979 s.54). A gain or loss may therefore accrue to the trustees although an election may be made to hold over the gain to the person taking the assets under Finance Act 1980 s.79 (as amended).

A similar market value rule applies on the termination (by virtue of death) of a life interest in possession in settled property, except that no chargeable gain accrues (because no capital gains tax is payable on death) except to the extent that assets were originally acquired by the trustees under a hold-over election.

## Value shifting

If control over a company is exercised in such a way that value passes out of shares in the company and passes into other shares, the transaction may be treated as one otherwise than by way of bargain made at arm's length and thereby market value would be taken (Capital Gains Tax Act 1979 ss.25, 26).

## 6 April 1965 market value

Capital gains tax was introduced with effect from 6 April 1965, and Capital Gains Tax Act 1979 Sch.5, para.12 provides an election for any gains to be calculated by reference to the market value on 6 April 1965 rather than the actual acquisition value on an earlier date (in which case a time apportionment of any gain would be allowed to remove the notional gain (or loss) made between the original date of acquisition and 6 April 1965).

## Reorganisation prior to 6 April 1965

If there has been a reorganisation (or take-over) before 6 April 1965 (excluding mere bonus issues) there is a mandatory deemed disposal and acquisition at 6 April 1965 at market value.

If a reorganisation takes place after 6 April 1965 a notional gain or loss is computed and this crystallises when an actual disposal takes place (Capital Gains Tax Act 1979 Sch.5, para. 14; Inland Revenue Statement of Practice SP 14/79).

## Negligible value

If shares have become of negligible value, the owner may claim for the shares to be treated as having been sold and immediately re-acquired for the value claimed. The Inspector of Taxes must be satisfied that the value has become negligible (Capital Gains Tax Act 1979 s.22(2)).

*Company ceasing to be a member of a group*

If a company leaves a group of companies it may be regarded as having sold and immediately acquired at market value an asset previously acquired from one of the group members (Taxes Act 1970 s.278). This is an anti-avoidance provision and would apply for instance if the company has received shares in another company that was previously owned by another group company and transferred under the hold-over provisions in Taxes Act 1970 s.273.

*Series of transactions*

Where there is a series of transfers of shares in a company to connected persons (as explained above) there is a requirement in Finance Act 1985 s.71 to aggregate the transfers made within the previous 6 years and take the market value of the aggregate number of shares and recalculate the value of the smaller transfers accordingly. This is an anti-avoidance provision to defeat the transfer of a large shareholding by occasional transfers of small holdings. Section 71 replaces Capital Gains Tax Act 1979 s.151, a more straightforward provision, which applied only to a series of transactions to the same person. Consequential market value rules are contained in Finance Act 1985 Sch. 21.

*Market value*

For capital gains tax purposes "market value" is defined in almost exactly the same terms as for capital transfer tax as "the price which those assets might *reasonably be expected to fetch* on a sale in the open market". There is to be no reduction in the estimated market value to reflect any market forces that would reduce the value because of flooding the market (Capital Gains Tax Act 1979 s.150).

Specifically in relation to unquoted shares or securities, in determining the market value it is to be assumed that, in the postulated open market there is available to any prospective purchaser all the information which a prudent prospective purchaser of the asset might reasonably require if he were proposing to purchase it from a willing vendor by private treaty and at arm's length. For a wider discussion, see 2.6 and 2.9.

Under the Capital Gains Tax Regulations (SI 1967 No 149), if there is a capital gains tax liability in point in respect of a transaction, any of the parties to the transaction can apply to the Commissioners of Inland Revenue, via an inspector of taxes, to determine the market value, provided there has been no tax appeal.

The determination of a market value on an appeal is final as between the Board, the inspector, parties to the appeal and third parties who were entitled to be joined in the appeal. Market value can also be finally determined if it was a material factor in an appeal notwithstanding that it was not in dispute. However, this does not apply where the question may be varied by a higher court or there has been fraud or wilful default.

A taxpayer and the Revenue cannot reach binding agreement on the value for capital gains tax purposes if a third party could be joined in the appeal, unless of course he does join in an agreement in writing or is given due notice and does not apply to be joined in the appeal.

Questions in dispute on an appeal against an assessment for capital gains tax or corporation tax on chargeable gains in respect of the value of land or of a lease of land are determined by the Lands Tribunal, and related questions of the value of unquoted shares or securities in a UK company are determined by the Special Commissioners (Taxes Management Act s.47).

## CTT and IHT (inheritance tax) valuation

The market value of an asset (whether in court proceedings or otherwise) for CTT or IHT purposes *on a death* is to be taken as the market value for capital gains tax purposes—this is for establishing the base cost to the recipient of the asset as there is no CGT on death.

Usually CTT/IHT reliefs—such as business assets relief—are ignored for CGT purposes, but it is understood that the CTT/IHT reliefs that recalculate the value of assets at death, such as in cases of dispositions within three years of death, will be taken into account for CGT valuation purposes (Capital Gains Tax Act 1979 ss.49, 153).

## 8.3 Capital transfer tax and inheritance tax

*Market value*

The definitions follow almost exactly the market value definitions for capital gains tax.

Market value is "the price which the property might reasonably be expected to fetch if sold in the open market ... but the price shall not be assumed to be reduced on the grounds that the whole property is to be placed on the market at one and the same time" (Capital Gains Tax Act 1984 s.160).

For unquoted shares "it shall be assumed that in that market there is available to any prospective purchaser of the shares ... all the information which a prudent prospective purchaser might reasonably require if he were proposing to purchase them from a willing vendor by private treaty and at arm's length" (Capital Gains Tax Act 1984 s.168).

Capital transfer tax (now inheritance tax) succeeded the old estate duty and many or most of the legal principles governing estate duty continue to govern capital transfer tax even though the whole thrust of the tax is different. In the case of *Crabtree* v *Hinchcliffe* Lord Justice Russell intimated that the principles of estate duty were the same as those applicable to capital gains tax; this can be extended to capital transfer tax and inheritance tax.

*Reduction in transferor's estate*

"... a transfer of value is any disposition made by (the transferor) as a result of which the value of his estate immediately after the disposition is less than it would be but for the disposition and the amount by which it is less is the value transferred by the transfer" (Capital Transfer Tax Act 1984 s.3(1)).

The foregoing has especial relevance, in the case of unquoted shares, to a disposal of shares out of a majority shareholding which results in the transferor retaining a minority shareholding only. The disparity in the valuations creates a larger CTT/IHT liability than would be the case if the transferred shares were capable of being valued in isolation. Note also that for CTT/IHT purposes the transfer of a minority interest out of a majority interest which is still a majority interest after the transfer will be valued effectively on the same basis as the majority interest because what is valued for CTT/IHT is the difference between the original holding and the reduced holding, both of which will be valued as a majority holding. Because of this there can be quite a disparity between the values for CTT/IHT and for CGT purposes even though exactly the same transfer is being valued.

The failure to exercise the right to take up a rights issue might result in a shareholding becoming of less value as against the remaining shares in the company, and this would constitute a diminution in the value of the transferor's estate.

### Related property

Where the value of shares in isolation is less than the value they would have if they and "related property" were valued together and that value was apportioned between them, the larger value is taken (Capital Transfer Tax Act 1984 s.161). Related property will include shares held by a spouse and a life interest trust (but not by sons or daughters).

### Associated operations

Where any two or more operations affect the same property, whether directly or indirectly, or are effected by reference to each other, they are deemed to have occurred at the same time—*the time of the latest such operation.* However, if an earlier operation gives rise to a transfer of value at that time the transfer of value deemed to take place when all the transactions are taken together is reduced by the earlier value. This is in the same vein as the capital gains tax provisions dealing with a series of transactions, but goes much wider (Capital Transfer Tax Act 1984 s.260).

## Close companies

Transfers of value made by a company are related back to the shareholders and are treated as net transfers, ie for CTT/IHT the "gift" is grossed-up. Any alteration in the share capital of an unquoted company or in the rights attaching thereto, is treated as a disposition made by the shareholders (Capital Transfer Tax Act 1984 ss.94, 85).

## Payment of CTT/IHT by instalments

Any CTT/IHT arising out of a transfer of shares or securities of a company on death which gave the deceased control of the company immediately before his death may be paid (under election) by instalments over eight and a half years. The instalment payment is also available if not less than 20% of the CTT/IHT is attributable to the value of shares.

## Business relief

Where the value transferred by a transfer of value is attributable to the value of any *relevant business property*, business relief may be available as follows:

*50%*
- shares or securities which gave the transferor control of the company;
- a business or interest in a business;

*30%*
- unquoted shares not giving control;
- land, buildings, machinery or plant used by a company controlled by the transferor or by a partnership of which he was a partner.

"Business" excludes investment and holding companies,

but, by virtue of the meaning of control (see below) ownership can be traced through intermediary companies including holding companies to the target company. The property must have been owned for (or replaced within) two years preceding the transfer (Capital Transfer Tax Act 1984 ss.103—114).

## Agricultural relief

For shares in a farming company, agricultural relief may be available, and this would take precedence over business relief.

Relief is 50% for controlling interests and 30% for minority interests. Agricultural relief applies to the land and buildings and business relief to other business assets. For agricultural relief the value of the agricultural property and assets is restricted to the value as if the property were subject to a perpetual covenant prohibiting use otherwise than as agricultural. This eliminates any development or hope value for CTT/IHT relief purposes.

"Where the whole or part of the value transferred is attributable to the value of shares in . . . a company it shall be taken . . . to be attributable . . . to the agricultural value of agricultural property . . . if the agricultural property forms part of the company's assets . . . and the shares gave the transferor control . . ." (Capital Transfer Tax Act 1984 ss.115—124).

## Control

For both business relief and agricultural relief "control" is through voting control. "A person has control at any time if he then has the control of powers of voting on all questions affecting the company as a whole which if exercised would yield a majority of the votes capable of being exercised thereon" (Capital Transfer Tax Act 1984 s.269).

## Death

Death is an occasion of charge for CTT/IHT, which is

charged as if, immediately before death, the individual made a transfer of value and the value transferred thereby had been equal to the value of his estate *immediately before his death.* So shares held by the deceased are valued for CTT/IHT immediately before death as part of his estate and related property is taken into account.

If the death itself causes a diminution in value of the shares—such as where the shareholder is also the source of the earnings of the company—then that diminution is treated as taking place immediately before the death (Capital Transfer Tax Act 1984 s.4).

## Surviving spouse exemption

If shares were left by a deceased person (who died before 13 November 1974) in trust for a surviving spouse, the shares will not suffer CTT/IHT on the death of the transferee. However, if that surviving spouse held other shares in the same company, in determining the value of those other shares the total holding would first be valued and then the pre-13 November 1973 value apportioned to eliminate those held in the surviving spouse trust (Capital Transfer Tax Act 1984 Sch.6, para.2).

## Settlements

Where shares are held in trust they will be regarded as forming part of the estate of a beneficiary who has an interest in possession (that is an entitlement to any of the income of the trust).

The termination of an interest in possession is treated as a transfer of value. Shares held by the settlement would be aggregated with any shares held in the free estate of the beneficiary (Capital Transfer Tax Act ss.49, 50).

Discretionary settlements are charged to CTT/IHT at 30% of the lifetime rates on each ten yearly anniversary from the creation of the trust falling after 31 March 1983 (Capital Transfer Tax Act 1984 ss.58—76).

There is no CTT/IHT charge on transfers of assets out of

an accumulation and maintenance settlement to the beneficiaries.

## 8.4 Income tax

*Share incentives and options*

Shares issued to an employee would normally be taxable under Schedule E on the market value (Taxes Act 1970 s.183 and *Weight* v *Salmon*) to the extent that market value exceeds the amount paid for the shares. For this purpose the legislation does not define market value and the general understanding of the words should probably prevail; any special importation of terms and conditions applying for other tax purposes—such as that requiring information to be assumed to be available to a prospective purchaser (Capital Gains Tax Act 1979 s.152; Capital Transfer Tax Act 1984 s.168) and the assumption that there is no discount for a disposal of all the shares at one time (Capital Gains Tax Act 1979 s.150; Capital Transfer Tax Act 1984 s.160)—would not apply. However, in practice it would probably be that the capital gains tax valuation rules would apply. See also *Ede* v *Wilson* (issue of shares at par); *Tyrer* v *Smart* (gift of shares to directors).

Share incentive scheme shares caught under Finance Act 1972 s.79 and treated as disposed of at the earliest occasion of seven years after the acquisition or cessation of any beneficial interest, or when shares cease to be subject to specified restriction, are deemed disposed of at market value, and a Schedule E tax charge arises on the excess of the then market value over the market value at the time of acquisition (Finance Act 1972 s.79). The capital gains tax market value rules apply (Finance Act 1972 Sch.12, para.6).

See also Finance Act 1976 s.67 for shares acquired partly paid and bought on instalment terms. Capital gains tax market value rules apply.

See Finance Act 1978 ss.53 to 61 as to profit-sharing schemes. Capital gains tax market value rules apply.

## Share options

A gain realised on the exercise of an option is the difference between "the amount that a person might reasonably expect to obtain from a sale in the open market at the time the shares are acquired and the consideration given for them or for the option" (Taxes Act 1970 s. 186).

As for s.183 (see above) no definition of market value is given, except that the market value on which tax is charged under Schedule E is to be taken as the acquisition cost for capital gains tax purposes. See also Finance Act 1980 Sch. 10 as to savings-related share option schemes. Capital gains tax market value rules would apply.

## Trading receipts

A capital receipt of a trader consisting of shares in exchange for some business interest or property is valued at open market value according to the capital gains tax rules *(Wolf Electric Tools Ltd* v *Wilson)*.

If the shares are received as trading income as a result of a sale or exchange, the money value, or market value of the shares would have to be ascertained and taken as at the end of the trader's accounting period. A discount may be available if the shares were not capable of being realised until a future time (but not to wipe out the value of shares on that basis alone) *(Gold Coast Selection Trust Ltd* v *Humphrey)*. This market value would be determined for income tax or corporation tax purposes only. There would not be a capital gains tax charge if a charge to income tax arises. See 8.7 below for a discussion of money value.

## Transactions in land

In relation to the Schedule D Case VI charge on gains arising from transactions in land—under Taxes Act 1970 s.488—including gains underlying a shareholding, "all such valuations shall be made as are appropriate to give effect to [section 488]" (Taxes Act 1970 s.489(6)(b)).

## 8.5 Stamp duty

Assets may be transferred between associated companies without giving rise to a stamp duty charge—see Finance Act 1930, s.42.

The sale of shares or a transaction involving the exchange of shares is liable to stamp duty as a conveyance or transfer on sale and therefore attracts *ad valorem* stamp duty. If the transaction forms part of a scheme of reconstruction, stamp duty relief under Finance Act 1986, s.77, and capital duty relief under Finance Act 1973 Sch.10, para.19 may be available.

Under the Stamp Act 1891 s.55, where the consideration, or any part of the consideration, for a conveyance on sale consists of any stock or marketable security, the conveyance is to be charged with *ad valorem* duty in respect of the value of the stock or security. Where assets of different character are agreed to be sold for one consideration for the whole, a *bona fide* apportionment of the consideration among the various assets is required to be made (following *West London Syndicate Ltd* v *IRC*).

The case of *John Foster & Sons* v *IRC* indicates that the value of the consideration is to be made by reference to the value of the property conveyed or transferred. See also *Carlyon Estate Ltd* v *IRC*.

In the case of *Stanyforth* v *IRC*, it was confirmed that the value of property conveyed is by reference to the value on sale in the open market.

It should be noted that for stamp duty valuation purposes the special prohibition against flooding the market and the assumption that information is to be available as on a sale by private treaty, are not present. This therefore allows a possible reduction in open market value in appropriate circumstances.

A sale at undervalue is stamped as a voluntary disposition (*Lap Shun Textiles Industrial Co Ltd* v *Collector of Stamp Revenue*).

## 8.6 Capital duty

Under Finance Act 1973 Sch.19, para.4, capital duty is

chargeable on the "actual" value of assets of any kind contributed by the members.

Actual value is not defined in the Finance Act 1973 but it is the expression used in the EEC Directive of 17 July 1979 to distinguish between nominal value and actual value. In the European Court of Justice Case No 161/78 (*P. Conradsen A/S* v *Ministry for Fiscal Affairs*), it was held that capital duty must be charged on the actual value of the assets contributed to a company and not on their book value. Additionally, it was suggested that potential tax liabilities chargeable on the profits of the company should not be taken into consideration.

## 8.7 Section 233 distributions

For the purposes of Taxes Act 1970 s.233 there is scant assistance in determining how the value of a distribution is to be arrived at. Under s.232 a company which makes a qualifying distribution shall, if the recipient so requests in writing, furnish to him a statement in writing showing "the amount or value of the distribution". Under s.233(3) in respect of a transfer of assets by a company to its members, the amount or value of the benefit received by a member is determined according to its market value. There is no such importation of market value concept in s.233(2)(b).

However, it is unlikely that it could be argued that the value of the distribution would be anything less than the value that the recipient could receive on realising it. Some assistance can be found in the case of *Gold Coast Selection Trust Ltd* v *Humphrey*, in which Viscount Simon said "if the asset is difficult to value but is nonetheless of a money value, the best valuation possible must be made". In that case he said that the fact that the asset could not be realised at once may reduce its present value although there was no reason for treating it for the purposes of income tax as though it had no value until it could be realised. He also made reference to the case where the assets take the form of fully paid shares, saying that the valuation would take into account the prospective yields, marketability, the general outlook for the type of business of the company which has allotted the shares and similar issues. However, the fact that a discount might be available because the shares could not necessarily be realised at once, and the absence of the prohibition against flooding the market and the absence of the requirement to assume information would be available to the potential purchaser, might remove the capital duty market value concept considerably away from the CGT and CTT/IHT market value concept.

The question also arises whether a distribution is to be valued in terms of the benefit received, or in terms of the value of the asset that is distributed, ie before or after any fragmentation. In the case of *Short* v *Treasury Commissioners* it was held that to impute a controlling interest valuation to a minority interest is not correct. Although this case may not be on all fours with the distribution of shares in a subsidiary company or other investment to members of the distributing company, it is likely that the same principle would apply to the distribution of a controlling interest in a subsidiary to a number of shareholders of the parent.

# Chapter 9

# The share valuation report

## 9.1 Introduction

An accurate valuation report of private company shares cannot be prepared without a full understanding of the purpose of the valuation, of the background to the valuation, of share valuation principles (Chapter 2) and of the company. The place to start from the practical point of view is with the person (individual or company) for whom the valuation is being carried out.

It is imperative to know whose shares are being valued, and to identify the full shareholding in the subject company belonging to that person (or persons), including shares of different classes, debentures and so on. In ascertaining the true value of any particular shareholding it may be necessary also to have regard to other securities or rights that the person has in or over the subject company (Chapter 3). Clearly, the relationship of the shareholder with the subject company must also be established — the shareholder may be a parent company, a director or simply an individual shareholder.

Having thus arrived at the starting post, the valuer can commence the exercise by assembling the necessary facts and documenting evidence ready for his eventual valuation report. The valuer's special position may, depending upon the size of the shareholding that is being valued and other circumstances, give him access to far more information than an ordinary purchaser of shares would have. The degree of information that would be available in the particular case should be decided upon (see 2.6), and the valuation report prepared accordingly, by reference to the following relevant matters.

## 9.2 Sources of information

Having established who the shareholder is, it is useful to schedule the initial sources of information. These will include the client, principal officers of the company and third party advisers such as estate agents or accountants or solicitors. The company accountant, and particularly the company secretary, are in a position to provide valuation information, as also may be long-term shareholders who are closely involved with the activities of the company.

## 9.3 Purpose of valuation

The valuation report must state clearly the purpose of valuation and should indicate which, if any, tax is in point and why. The identity and number of shares should be given, and the date for which the valuation is given. At all times, in respect of all matters concerning the valuation, the date is of fundamental importance (2.8), and facts and figures which cannot be substantiated as at that date will always be suspect. In practical terms this can give rise to serious difficulties, for example, where the date of valuation falls, say, halfway through a company's accounting period.

The balance sheet at the end of that period cannot be taken automatically as a reflection of the state of affairs of the company as at the date the valuation is required. The same can be said of the company's trading profits for that year. It is necessary to see what has happened during the year and it would be usual to take the balance sheet at the end of the previous year and amend that accordingly to take account of events occurring between that date and the date of the valuation. It is not always a practical possibility, however, and sometimes it is necessary to compromise by apportioning increases in value or profits that have been made over the year on a time basis. Even so, Shares Valuation Division may take issue with apportionments that are made arbitrarily. It will rather depend upon the facts in each case, and indeed the scale of the valuation.

## 9.4 The subject company

Obviously, it is necessary to identify the subject company, its business address and registered office, and its professional advisers, and the valuer must also have a knowledge of the company's trading history. To some extent these may be taken from the directors report on the annual accounts, but very often this is rather brief and a more detailed knowledge is required, especially if there has been any material change in the trading activities, particularly any notable cyclical trends. Any parent and subsidiary companies must be identified and their relationship fully understood; the capital structure of each company must be noted and the shareholding identified. The valuer must understand whether or not he is valuing shares from trading results taken from consolidated accounts, and wherever subsidiary companies are involved the valuation exercise requires an individual inspection of each subsidiary and cognisance of its impact on the parent and the parent's activity and value. A schedule of parent, subsidiary and associated companies and their capital structures should be prepared, and inter-company trading activities, guarantees, debts etc noted.

A schedule of the capital structure of the subject company must be prepared and the shares which are the subject of the valuation identified in the context of this structure (3.1, 3.5). Such a schedule could also be the base for identifying previous transactions (sales, acquisitions, bonus or rights issues and other transfers (2.15)). Any known prices would be recorded here and the valuer must ensure that any transactions that would appear to be material to the valuation of the shares in the current circumstances are brought into account.

A full list of shareholders should be made and so far as

possible previous shareholders identified and brought into the schedule. This may have relevance for capital gains tax and capital transfer tax/inheritance tax purposes, especially if there have been transactions between connected parties or members of the same family (8.2 and 8.3). For this purpose all shareholders' relationships with each other should be identified, not only family relations, but also any trusteeships, nominee holdings and company or director connections.

This will enable decisions to be taken as to whether there are any groupings of shares to be made for the purpose of valuation under the various tax rules which deal with related party transactions, and may be relevant in identifying whether somebody has *de facto* control (such as where a person holds shares on his own account, and also as trustee, and the holdings together constitute effective control (3.3)).

## 9.5 Basis of valuation

At some stage in bringing the information together, a decision has to be taken by the valuer as to which basis of valuation is appropriate — whether dividend basis, earnings basis, assets basis or hybrid basis. The probability is that by looking at the size of the shareholding in question, the trading activities of the company and the net asset backing, the valuer will have come to an early decision as to what basis would be appropriate (see 3.7).

In any valuation report (as distinct from an "opinion" of value as discussed at 1.2 and 2.10) the basis must be stated and the reasons for choosing the basis explained. It is certainly not unknown for the valuer to change his mind as to the appropriate basis once he has immersed himself in the detail of the valuation. For example, in looking at the current (that is at the date of valuation) trading activities of the company, the valuer may consider the directors are carrying on the business with insufficient funds with the result that an initial view that, say, a dividend basis applies, is put aside in favour of an asset value on a break-up basis. As long as a firm decision on the valuation basis is eventually made and explained in the final valuation report, there is no reason why the valuer should not leave open the question of which basis to adopt until quite late in his examination. Indeed, apart from having an astute mind, one of a valuer's greatest assets is an open mind. He should be wary of first impressions and should not be influenced by any preconceived idea that the client may have concerning the value of the shares or the viability or otherwise of the company.

## 9.6 Statutory rules

It is certainly most helpful to the valuer to identify those statutory rules that are pertinent to the valuation, and schedule and re-read them before commencing the valuation itself. If he is not well versed in taxation he would do well to seek confirmation of the rules that will or may apply. These can normally be set out in fairly short terms and it is hoped that Chapter 8, dealing with taxation, will help in respect to this.

The valuation report should contain the tax valuation sections for the avoidance of doubt and it also helps to list those valuation concepts to which the valuer has had regard in putting together his valuation. Similarly, any company law requirements, such as the valuation rules under Companies Act 1985 ss.103 and 104 in relation to the issue of shares for non-cash consideration, should be referred to.

A suggested form for setting out such principles is given in the model valuation report in Appendix 1.

## 9.7 Memorandum and Articles of Association

Most companies use standard forms of Memorandum and Articles of Association and these usually draw on the standard clauses in Tables A, D or E as set out in the Companies Act (3.2). It can be useful to have a summary of the company's main objects clause but it is particularly important that the pre-emption articles are recorded. Any other restrictions on transfer of shares, along with any special articles concerning casting votes and the like, should also be recorded.

Any restriction on share transfer clause is particularly important because of the discounts usually given from quoted company comparisons for the private company shareholding which is subject to such restrictions (2.13). Any change in rights must certainly be checked and, if currently relevant, stated in the valuation report.

Also to be recorded would be any shareholders' agreement in relation to profit distributions as this may have a material effffect on the rights of shareholders (3.4). It is likely that Shares Valuation Division will not accept that any shareholders' agreement exists without some evidence.

Any special resolutions that have an effect on rights of members should also be noted. It is unlikely that other minutes will be relevant to a valuation report.

## 9.8 Financial and management background

The real detail of the valuation commences with a review of the financial and management background of the subject company. At this point it is worth reiterating that the valuer is in a privileged position in terms of having access to company records and accounts and statutory books. It is most unlikely that much information beyond that which is in the hands of a shareholder would be made available to any prospective purchaser (2.6).

A director is under no obligation to disclose confidential company information to anyone, including the company's shareholders, and therefore the information drawn upon for the purposes of the valuation report should be weighed in relation to the impact that that information would have on any price offered for the shares. If the information would be material in this respect, the valuer should determine whether it would or would not become available to that purchaser and determine the value accordingly.

By way of example, the existence of a possible takeover bid by one company for another may have a material effect on the share value of the latter. If the valuer discovers that, as a matter of fact, this information, whilst known to the directors is not known to anyone else, there would be no reason to reflect this potential bid in the value of a minority interest, unless it could be said that in the circumstances of the case a "reasonable" director would divulge that information without jeopardising the affairs of the company in any way. In the case of a controlling interest, or of the whole shareholding, this question becomes rather more sensitive and the valuer would need to satisfy himself as to whether, as a matter of fact, this information would be generally available on any sort of investigation by the purchaser, having regard to the fact that disclosure of the information by the directors would not take place if the disclosure might prejudice the interest of the company (see 2.6).

Again, it is worth pointing out that the financial and management information to be investigated is for the purpose of establishing a value as at the date for valuation. There is therefore little point in taking steps to find out about events happening after the date for valuation if there was no forewarning of such events before that date.

## 9.9  Balance sheet and annual accounts

The annual accounts, including the balance sheet, will contain the directors' reports and auditors' certificates, and between them these will set out some of the information required for the purposes of the valuation. If at all possible, accounts and balance sheets for the five years prior to the date for valuation should be collected and copies put on the valuation file. It can often be helpful to have copies of these accounts appended to the valuation report. Although this may not be strictly necessary, it indicates that the approach to the valuation is based on collecting and displaying all the appropriate evidence.

It helps to have all the background information on which

the valuation report is being prepared kept in one file, together with correspondence between the valuer and all other parties, including Shares Valuation Division, as this will help considerably if negotiation with the Inland Revenue is drawn out over a number of months.

The directors' report may be useful for getting a "first feel" for the company's affairs but there is very little consistency between directors' reports of different companies and the valuer should obviously expect to look well beyond the directors' report on the accounts. The audit report also attached to the accounts should be read as this will identify whatever reservations exist in the mind of the auditor concerning the accounting and reporting quality of the company. If there is a qualified audit report then, depending upon the seriousness of it, the valuer will be careful in evaluating unsubstantiated statements made by directors of the company.

The accounts will also include a Statement of Source and Application of Funds and this is useful for understanding the balance sheet changes that have occurred during the period for which the accounts have been prepared. In particular it may help identify material changes in, for example, stocks, debtors, creditors and bank balances during that period.

If current cost accounts are also prepared the valuer may wish to inspect them, but it is important to compare like with like, and historic cost based figures should not be confused with current cost based figures. It may be safest, unless current cost accounts have been prepared for a number of years, to restrict the investigation to the historic cost accounts and to make any necessary projections by reference to those.

It is useful to prepare a summary of the trading and profit and loss accounts over the period under review, and this summary would show the turnover plus other income and gains, providing a total earnings figure per the profit and loss account. The summary would also give the net profit and loss and, at some stage, into this schedule can be inserted notes relating to extraordinary or exceptional items shown in the accounts and which, for the purpose of arriving at "ordinary" net trading profits, will be added back or removed from the profit and loss account figure shown.

The schedule is also a useful place to record the Retail Price Index figures for the balance sheet date and also at the date for valuation. By adjusting all the results by reference to the RPI one will be able to see the company performance in the context of present day values, which is vital for making any sort of estimate as to present day value of future maintainable profit (see the Model Valuation in Appendix 1).

A summary of balance sheets as such is probably of little value because a valuation exercise must look at market value of assets at the date for the valuation and not at net book values. However, it can be useful to see the relationship between the market value of business assets and the market value of non-business assets. By comparing the movement in the ratio of one against the other, an underlying movement may emerge that may help the valuer judge the company's state of health. For example, if the percentage of investment assets as against business assets is continuing to fall, this may indicate a long term decline in the company's ability to cushion itself against adverse trading conditions. A trend the other way might well suggest that additional asset value should be brought into the valuation, whether or not the indications are that another basis is appropriate for the basic valuation. This schedule can be difficult to produce because it necessitates revaluing the balance sheet for each year under review. There is certainly no point in doing this unless one can identify assets on the balance sheet that could be regarded as not strictly required for business purposes.

In terms of exceptional and extraordinary items, some of the most common exceptional items are pension fund payments on or around the setting-up of a self-administered pension fund, and the sale or purchase of investments, but the valuer should watch for other unexpected items, such as heavy removal costs relating to a once-and-for-all move to new premises.

169

## 9.10 Dividend policy

Any dividend policy (see Chapter 4) of the company must be ascertained and the criteria set down on paper so that the valuer understands fully what that policy is. The dates of previous dividend payments should be listed and the pre- and post- tax figures shown. This is of particular importance where minority interests are being valued. Whether or not a dividend policy is being followed it is necessary to determine the company's current and future cash requirements because, just as a history of no dividends can come to an end, so too can a history of dividend payments. It is difficult to foresee a future change in a policy that is already established, but any management projections which show either a deficit or surfeit of cash in the future will be an important indicator of an impending change, and this fact should be recorded.

## 9.11 Management projections and profit forecasts

The balance sheet and accounts will provide the historic facts. Current management projections and profit forecasts, provided they have been prepared on proper accounting principles, will be of great value in projecting those historic results forward. More often than not in the case of a going concern, the valuer will be trying to establish future maintainable profits, and therefore management accounts and forecasts based on sound accounting records can be very valuable in, if nothing else, establishing a reasonably acceptable view of the current position. Once again, it is important to stress that one is looking at the date for valuation. It is pointless to bring in as evidence any management forecasts, budgets and so on made after this date, unless it is reasonably certain that that information was available at the date for valuation. If there are budgets prepared regularly then a comparison of past budgets and management accounts with the actual financial audited accounts could be useful to see how accurate the projections and forecasts are.

## 9.12 Directors and personnel

It has been proved time and again that a company's trading position, its goodwill, its profit-earning capacity and its growth, are continuous hostages of management. A company, a business, a venture is as successful as the persons carrying it on. It is not uncommon to find that the private company is shareholder controlled and directed and its success depends upon its business goodwill in a locality or narrow specialism, often depending upon a personal relationship between the shareholder director and one or a few other parties. That is not to say that such a company has no value, but in the author's view, if the company's business is so personal to the shareholder director, there is much doubt that a dividends or earnings basis may be applied (see 6.19; 6.20).

The valuer should prepare his own management review identifying the age and experience of each director and any specialist knowledge or qualification the person may have. He should consider that information against the business being carried on. For example, if, in a property development company, he discovered half a dozen directors all aged between 20 and 25, no one of those directors having any experience of property transactions and having no qualification in relation to property, then the valuer must seriously question the likelihood of success.

It is useful to point out that the valuer is not concerned with the potential of the business if it were subjected to major change; the valuer is projecting the *status quo* forward at the date for the valuation. The value of the company stems from that, at least initially. When looking at the market for the shares in the particular company it may be necessary to modify this view (see, eg, 2.11).

In the summary of management personnel should be included current remuneration and brief details of any service contracts and their unexpired period. This may be of particular importance in the case of key executives; any "keyman" insurance policies will help identify such individuals. Directors' remuneration would be listed along with pension contributions and benefit packages, which in many cases can be quite substantial. Not to be forgotten is any "golden handshake" or redundancy liability on a future termination of employment.

It is imperative to record any agreement for the sale or transfer of shares, or subscription for new shares, to or by any directors or employees. A copy of any share option/ incentive scheme arrangement must be obtained and the impact of such schemes taken into account, obviously to identify what sort of dilution in existing share values there may be.

A brief summary of the company's employees might also be obtained, and, if at all possible, a review of staff level changes made, especially if the business is labour intensive. Trade Union agreements or other workforce agreements should be inspected. If it is discovered that the company uses outside workers, it would be useful to check that control of such a workforce is properly conducted; a particular problem at this time is the company's responsibilities under PAYE regulations, and the valuer might like to satisfy himself that "home-workers" and other "casuals" are not, in reality, employees with the result that the company may have built up PAYE liabilities and penalties.

The company's pension scheme or schemes, especially small self-administered schemes, should be examined to identify what level of contributions have been made and will be made in the future and whether there is any other connection between the company and the pension scheme. For example, property occupied by the company may be owned by the fund and the valuer may wish to ensure that the fund has received all the necessary approvals from the Superannuation Funds Office.

## 9.13 Tax computations

Along with a review of the accounts, the valuer should inspect corporation tax returns. It may also be necessary to examine other tax returns for which the company is responsible, to ensure that it is meeting the requirements relating to PAYE and deduction of tax at source in respect of interest, royalties, dividend payments. There may be hidden contingent liabilities if these responsibilities have not been observed. In particular, the valuer should ensure that all VAT matters are up to date and there are no disputes. Equally, corporation tax affairs should be checked to ensure there are no points in dispute, especially in relation to any unused tax losses and balancing adjustments in respect of plant, machinery or, industrial buildings.

## 9.14 Assets and real estate

A schedule must be prepared of all assets owned by the company and a note made to explain the uses to which the assets are put in the company. The assets' current market value must be determined (6.6 *et seq*) and in the case of a going concern the valuer must see whether there is any extraordinary value attaching to business assets which might identify a particular strength in the asset-backing of the business. He must also identify any valuable assets standing to one side of the business assets, which may perhaps indicate that a dividend policy will have to be instituted at some future time.

If the company has a plant register it should be inspected. It should show the depreciation policy and identify whether plant is obsolete or not, indicating whether plant is likely to be replaced in the near future. The current value of plant and machinery in the case of a going concern probably will not enter into the valuation except in the unusual circumstance of a going concern business being valued on an asset basis rather than an earnings basis. In the event of likely liquidation, the valuer will be seeking to establish the break-up basis (6.2) and some advice may have to be taken either from the company directors themselves,, or, more probably, from outside experts, as to the likely value of the plant and machinery on a break-up basis or in a forced sale.

If plant and machinery accounts for a substantial part of the value of the company, then it would certainly be advisable to obtain an outside opinion as to what the sale value might be. Otherwise, subject to the valuer's opinion, it might be perfectly acceptable to make his own estimate of what the assets might realise on such a sale, taking into account the costs of the sale and the use to which the purchaser would put the assets, and bearing in mind that the purchaser may be planning to sell on the assets and would require a profit himself. The more specialist the equipment the more necessary it will be to look for specialist assistance.

Included in the schedule of assets should be any that are not actually shown on the balance sheet, the most common of which is usually goodwill (6.19), but only if there is such an asset that stands within the company as opposed to attaching to the actual business that the company is carrying on, ie the actual share valuation itself will reflect ultimately the goodwill in the under-taking being carried on by the company. However, there may be other assets, including copyrights, with undisclosed value attaching. The valuer must therefore look for any patents, trade marks, registered designs, publications, technical designs, computer programs, recordings etc. Any contracts and agreements should be inspected and the importance of the "asset" to the business and the company must be ascertained. It is very likely that outside expertise will have to be used in the process of ascertaining the value or confirming a value given by the company directors. If the valuer can see that the goodwill attaching to any such asset is already reflected in the earnings of the company, it will probably not be necessary to ascribe an independent value because that will be reflected in the capitalisation of the earnings of the company.

All other assets should be scheduled, including properties. In the case of leasehold there may also be obligations which must be ascertained. In a property portfolio, it will certainly be necessary for a professional valuation to be undertaken by a firm of property valuers, who will also be able to value any leasehold obligations. It should not be overlooked that this will involve expense and the valuer would do well to ensure that provision has been made to meet his costs and the costs of third parties.

## 9.15 Liabilities

In addition to liabilities in respect of leasehold interests, mentioned above, there may be other liabilities, contingent or otherwise, and a schedule of these should be prepared. In the case of an asset value in contemplation of the liquidation of the company, there may be redundancy payment obligations, pension payments to be made, and contract cancellation penalties.

Any current litigation should be looked into and the possible outcome considered in terms of the effect on the company. Expenditure commitments should also be considered; these may include research and development costs that are expected to continue into the future, or perhaps are expected to start at some future time (but only if as a consequence of current activities and commitments). Ongoing construction costs may be relevant and there may be stage payments required under existing contracts with outside parties.

## 9.16 Order book

If available, the valuer should look at the order book at the time for the valuation, and compare that with the past performance of the company, looking particularly for cancellations through lack of delivery, or any other fall, or indeed increase, of orders. An increase in unfulfilled orders may indicate not only that demand is growing, but that the company is unable to meet the orders in time. That failure may be due to under-capitalisation, labour disputes, out-moded machinery or bad management. Any material change in past trading activities should be identified and explanations obtained from management. Such changes could be in product or method of production, type of customer or type of outlet. Any change, especially in the recent past, may indicate that the historic trading performance may bear little relevance to future activities and future maintainable earnings.

## 9.17 Suppliers, joint ventures and third party commitments

It is always useful to know the number of suppliers to the company as this may indicate strength or weakness. For example, a supplier of widgets who has all his widgets turned by the only widget-turner in the world clearly is exposed in commercial terms and may be a hostage to the fortunes of the one and only widget-turner. A principal requirement for a healthy company is that suppliers of important commodities should be capable of being replaced easily and quickly. If this is not the case then there must be some risk factor.

Joint ventures, franchise arrangements and other third party commitments, especially of any size, should be examined to identify their relevance to the trading activities of the company and the importance to the profit-earning potential and growth of the company. In these cases there are likely to be contracts or agreements which should be read. Joint ventures may carry continuing liabilities. There may therefore be a negative value attaching to a joint venture if it has not been carried on for a sufficient time to show a return. The identity of the joint venture parties may be relevant and of course the full terms of the arrangement must be understood and noted in the valuation report if appropriate.

## 9.18 Bad debts

To get an idea of the risk attaching to the company's business it can be useful to look at the bad debts over a period of years. In the case of a company approaching liquidation it may also help to indicate what problems will exist in collecting money from debtors. A list, as at the date for valuation, of aged debtors and creditors should be prepared, and in the case of debtors it should identify which are bad and which are doubtful. Debts which are older than the average trade terms normally found in the particular type of business should be investigated to see whether they will turn bad, and the reasons for that should be ascertained.

## 9.19 Foreign trading and currency exposure

Any foreign subsidiaries or branch operations should be examined in the same way as the company's UK trade and business is investigated. Obviously it is more difficult to investigate activities overseas and in appropriate circumstances a visit to the foreign location may be necessary. In fact, the valuer should almost invariably visit the premises of a company whose shares he is valuing. Despite the inconvenience or costs that may be involved, this principle must also apply in respect of overseas businesses.

Currency exposure is a problem of growing relevance as international trade increases. Many businesses now conduct their entire trade in $US and convert into £ sterling for accounting purposes. This tends to have no real risk factor attaching. The difficulty arises where trade is being carried on in more than one currency and debtors and creditors exist in differing currencies. Here the valuer should pay particular attention to protective measures that the company may or may not be taking in terms of currency exposure. Where any sizeable amount of the company's funds is tied up in foreign currency, whether long term or on a continuing short-term basis, the valuer may have to introduce into his valuation a risk factor to reflect the danger of a sudden currency fluctuation that could cost the company dearly, yet does not arise out of its normal trading activities.

## 9.20 Financial rates and data

It is useful as at the date for valuation to identify various data relating both to the company and to general economic conditions. Whether or not a quoted company comparison is to be used it is useful to take the FT Actuaries Share Index for the appropriate industry sector as at the date for valuation, and show the index figure for the date twelve months previously. Also the FT Share Index for those dates can be given. Clearing banks base rate is useful, as is the yield on undated gilts and often the rate of exchange against the $US.

In terms of the company financial data the various ratios which may be listed for the purpose of assessing the subject company are:

*The credit ratio:* This is the ratio of trade creditors to trade purchases. A high credit ratio indicates that the company is, for good or ill, extracting the maximum patience from its suppliers.

*The debtor ratio:* This is the ratio of debtors to sales. A high debtor ratio shows that the company is having some difficulty in collecting debts from its customers.

*Creditor debtor comparison:* A high credit ratio and a low debtor ratio indicate *prima facie* that the company is maximising its trade related cash flow. A high debtor ratio and low credit ratio indicates the opposite and indeed could point to cash flow difficulties.

*Turnover of stock:* The rate of turnover of stock is a very valuable indicator of the success of the business and many trade associations publish average stock turnover rates. The rate is determined by dividing the cost of sales by the average of stock levels. The cost of sales is the annual purchases plus opening stock figure, less the closing stock figure, and will also include any manufacturing costs or added value.

*Return on capital:* The return on capital is considered to be an important piece of information, calculated by dividing the pre-tax net profits by the average net value of capital employed multiplied by 100. Many factors can create a distortion in this figure and it would be quite dangerous simply to take the return on capital at the date for valuation by reference to the net worth at that time and current estimated net profit. Reference must also be made to long-term and short-term cyclical trends as well as short-term distortions in trading activities.

*The ratio of assets to liabilities:* Ignoring fixed assets and shareholders reserves, this is a useful ratio for identifying whether, by reference to the movement in the ratio over a period of months or years, there is a sufficiency of working capital. Any suggestion that additional working capital is required is likely to have an adverse effect on the value of the shares.

*The liquid asset ratio:* this is a similar ratio to the ratio of assets to liabilities but excludes stocks. If current liabilities exceed current assets it indicates that the company is unable to meet its current debts without realising the value of assets. This may well indicate a serious trading problem, or indeed insolvency.

*Dividend cover:* This is the ratio of the earnings to the dividend yield. The dividend cover shows the number of times that the net dividend can be paid out of current net earnings. A high cover indicates considerable security for future dividends; low cover leads to less certainty that the dividend can be maintained.

## 9.21 Future trading prospects and special factors

It is necessary to have from the company's management not only profit forecasts but their views on the future trading prospects of the company in the context of the general economic climate. Any special factors relating to the company, the trade or the industry should be noted. For example, a company in the transport industry may in fact be a specialist business dealing with the transportation of heavy engineering items. The company may not be trading in any other area. It may also be that the directors know of a forthcoming decline in the transport industry generally, but have reason to believe the transportation of heavy engineering items is and will continue to be stable.

## 9.22 Supporting documentation

As has been mentioned, a share valuation report should be supported by whatever documentation is available. By way of reminder the following may be appended with advantage to the valuation report:

- accounts and balance sheet for the past (5) years;
- independent valuations of real estate or other assets;

179

- copy of Memorandum and Articles of Association;
- pertinent minutes and resolutions;
- copies of material contracts which are referred to in the share valuation report;
- schedules of financial data;
- signed statements by any party certifying any particular facts or figures.

## 9.23 General economic outlook

The company's management should be able to direct the valuer to a range of publications and a variety of information relating to the general economic outlook for the company and its trade. In addition to the information so provided, the valuer should seek independent views, and a particularly valuable source would be trade associations and trade journals. If the names of competitors and companies carrying on comparable businesses can be identified, further information can be gleaned from the Extel Card System (from Extel Statistical Services Ltd). Information relating to quoted companies can be had from Datastream International Limited, and much information on a range of economic and trade matters can be obtained from the Department of Trade and Industry.

It is important to identify the place of the subject company in the context of its general economic surroundings, which are undoubtedly bound to have an effect on the value of the business as a going concern.

## 9.24 Valuation approach

By the time the valuer has gathered all the above details, he will have a good idea of how he intends to approach his valuation; where he thinks the emphasis should be placed in terms of the proper basis of valuation; whether he will need to adopt a hybrid basis approach; whether he must take into account any particular quirk in the asset-base or earnings of the company; and what facts he expects to give special weight, and maybe what facts he intends to ignore.

He may, for example, decide to ignore the fact that a particular product that was developed by the subject company during the year, which proved a total failure in all respects and has cost a great deal of money, should not unduly influence the future prospects for the company; perhaps because the individual who devised the product is no longer with the company. This may be of sufficient moment to note in the valuation report, and equally it would be of sufficient moment to note that the results of the exercise are to be removed from the assessment of future maintainable earnings.

The valuation approach is very much a statement of the valuer's experience brought to bear on the subject company. It is likely to be regarded by Shares Valuation Division as opinion and may be attacked as such. Nevertheless, it is valid as such, for more than one judge will admit that a valuation is often no more than an arbitration of opinions.

### 9.25 Comparisons

As mentioned in 9.23, if any comparisons, whether with quoted companies or other companies, can be made, they should be brought into the valuation report, and any distinctions noted. If one uses a comparable company, then almost inevitably the comparison needs to be justified. More often than not, if a private company is being compared with a public quoted company, one would be concerned to identify the almost inevitable divergences. This is a most important area and it is the area where the valuer can expect to have most difficulty with Shares Valuation Division if opinions differ. The quoted company or other company comparison must therefore be undertaken with great care. The matter is considered in some detail in Chapters 4 and 5.

### 9.26 Calculation

Eventually, the valuer comes to the actual calculation.

Just as the data has been presented in the valuation report, so the calculation must be set out in unambiguous terms and should be capable of being followed through by someone who has not been a party to detailed examination of the affairs of the company. The figures used must be capable of easy reconciliation with the accounts, independent valuations and comparisons with other companies. A valuation report is a working document and should be quite explicit, starting with a basic statement of figures, showing calculations for values that are to be taken into a final calculation, giving reasons why particular figures or fractions or percentages are being used.

The eventual valuation on a per share basis may then have to be adjusted according to any tax rules that are pertinent, for example, CTT/IHT reliefs. It may well be that the actual calculation of the value chargeable to one or other of the taxes is then worked out by someone other than the valuer.

## 9.27 Review

When the valuer has determined his value and any tax liability or other consequence has been identified, it is wise to have the entire valuation report reviewed by another person. Having been involved in depth in a complicated share valuation, small points can easily be missed and it is clearly preferable to find those errors before the valuation report is submitted to the client or to the Inland Revenue.

## 9.28 Summary

In summary, the major decisions the valuer will have to make relate to the required yield or the price-to-earnings ratio; the weighting to be given in a hybrid valuation; and the discounts, whether from the PER of the quoted company comparison, or to reflect the lack of marketability of a private company's shares.

It is not constructive to choose a deliberately high or low

figure simply because one expects the "opposition" to take the other extreme and negotiate towards a point mid-way between the two. Such positioning gives weight to confrontational bargaining at the expense of what should be essentially a highly professional and absolute determination. A fully considered opinion is more easily adhered to through lengthy negotiations with the Revenue, and is less likely to engender polarisation of views.

# Chapter 10

# Dealing with Shares Valuation Division

Shares Valuation Division (SVD) is a department of the Capital Taxes Office of the Inland Revenue. The address of the Division is Rockley Road, London W14 0DF (telephone (01) 603 4622).

## 10.1 Introduction

The usual procedure is that the department responsible for making the tax assessment will request the taxpayer's valuation, and then pass it and the task of subsequent negotiation of agreed value to SVD. In cases involving land (as noted elsewhere in this book) SVD will refer subsidiary valuation points concerning land values to the appropriate District Valuer. Unfortunately, this often leads to additional delay in agreeing final figures, although it should not prevent the two sides agreeing other elements in the valuation, leaving the matter open to final adjustment when the land value has been agreed. This may not always be the most prudent course of action, however, particularly if the land value is significant in relation to the share valuation.

Shares Valuation Division maintains a file for every company in which is noted any agreed 6 April 1965 value (for capital gains tax purposes relevant for acquisitions of chargeable assets prior to that date), details of previous valuations of shares in the company and other facts and figures.

184

The valuation question may be referred to SVD whether or not the taxpayer has provided his own detailed valuation. The SVD will in the first place scrutinise each referral to see whether enough information is available to enable a valuation to be examined properly, and the department may request the taxpayer to complete a form VAL38 (VAL39 for preference shares or debentures). This is an enquiry form requesting the most basic share valuation information:

(1) What is the precise nature of the company's business?

(2) Is the company public or private?

(3) (a) What value is placed on the shares?
    (b) "Please furnish a full explanation of value(s) placed on the shares with supporting evidence"
    (c) By whom was the valuation made?

(4) A request for copies of Balance Sheet, Trading and Profit & Loss Accounts, Directors' Reports and Chairman's Statements for (x) years

(5) (a) What net dividends per share have been paid prior to the valuation date
    (b) When were the interim and fixed dividends for the last year paid?
    (c) What dividends were paid before the date of valuation in respect of the year(s) then current.

(6) Details (date, number and price) of those share sales nearest the date of valuation

(7) Details of share allotments near the date of valuation.

## 10.2 Agreed values — without prejudice

If sufficient information is available the SVD procedure is to decide first whether the particular valuation can be agreed without negotiation. This is not always an unconditional acceptance of the valuation by SVD but may well be a without prejudice agreement — which means that if another valuation incident arises, SVD is not bound to settle the subsequent valuation by reference to the "without prejudice" valuation. This procedure may be adopted in cases where the value or the tax charge is of little moment and where protracted negotiation may be of little benefit to either party.

It might also be where, for commercial reasons, a valuation must be adopted with immediate effect — such as for share option scheme purposes. Here a value may well be agreed promptly — but only for the purposes of a Schedule E charge under the appropriate charging provision.

A without prejudice valuation may also be agreed after prolonged negotiation where disagreement exists between the parties, but neither wishes to take the matter to the Commissioners. The agreement of a "without prejudice" valuation can also enable the taxpayer to negotiate a subsequent valuation without using the previous value as an established fact of value at that time. On balance, the author's view is that a without prejudice valuation should usually be regarded as an unsatisfactory expedient.

## 10.3 Size of shareholding

Shares Valuation Division will certainly base its choice of valuation basis on the size of the shareholding that is being valued. The standard approach is set out at 3.7.

The first reaction from SVD in any sizeable case is likely to be a statement, setting out the valuation basis they consider appropriate and the value derived therefrom. If, as is very possible, the valuer's report has been rejected, it is up to the valuer himself to put up a secondary attack by restating his valuation approach and explaining where and how this approach is realistic, always drawing on the evidence that has been supplied with the valuation report.

In particular, difficulty may be experienced if the valuer is putting a low dividend-basis value on an influential minority holding (25+%). SVD is more inclined towards an earnings bias — the only, but perhaps significant, power that a 25+% but less than 50% shareholding has is the power to maintain the *status quo* by blocking a special resolution put to the shareholders. Sometimes, the Articles of Association or a shareholders agreement may allow the holder of a specified percentage of shares to appoint a representative to the board of directors and this may also have some significance in the valuation agreement.

Whatever difficulties may arise, the share valuer must continue to negotiate in the knowledge that he has applied share valuation principles and presented the facts and evidence fully and impartially and, in the absence of error, that must be a successful approach.

## 10.4 Discounts

Another matter for dispute between valuer and SVD is the question of what discount to allow in any or all of the following areas:

- *Discount for lack of marketability* (see 2.16). This discount is usually given at the end of the valuation and is intended to reflect the *financial* measure of the disadvantage of holding shares which are subject to restrictions on transfer. SVD will take the view that minority shareholdings will be entitled to a greater discount than majority share-holdings — provided that this factor has not also entered into the equation when the earnings capitalisation (5.7) or the yield (4.8) for the share-holding was determined.

  The discount applied by the valuer should be justifiable, because SVD will have a firm view on the subject and a good deal of experience in arguing the point.

- *Notional dividends* (see 4.4-6). If a notional dividend stream has to be calculated, a discount from the dividend so determined should be given to reflect the fact that no dividends have actually been paid. This is usually accepted to be 50%, but SVD has been known to baulk at this on occasion, and might be expected to do so if the minority shareholding exceeds 25%.

- *Discounts from quoted and other PERs and Yields* (see 5.5, 4.8). Such discounts do not represent the lack of marketability of the shares but are a measure of the economic and profile difference between chosen comparisons and the subject company. They must be argued through, or at least be reasonable. The alternative to discounting is simply to take a smaller PER or a larger yield, but there is no real difference between the two approaches.

- *Break-up value discount* (see 6.2). On a total break-up of the company's assets, the valuer would identify the market value of the disposable and realisable assets, and discount this by 33 1/3% for the 50% shareholder. This discount may be less in some cases, but it depends not so much on the size of the shareholding as on the quality of the assets.

  For shareholdings greater than 50% this discount must fall, but at least 15% must be allowed, because of the risk factors attendant on a purchase (even of 100% of the company) in liquidating a company and realising the potential cash.

## 10.5 Yields

Inland Revenue rules-of-thumb are that for companies whose net worth is around £150,000, a dividend basis of up to 15% may be acceptable and an earnings yield in the order of 35% to 40% if dividends are payable, or 50% if not payable. In terms of Price to Earnings ratio, this is in the range of 2.5:1 to 2:1.

Above that net worth, PERs start at about 3:1, or the FTASI yield might be used as a basis and multiplied by, say, 2 for net worth up to £500,000, by 1.5 between £500,000 and £1,000,000, and taken as published for net worth above £1,000,000.

These are merely guidelines, to be viewed as a possible SVD starting point in their own deliberations, and should be reflected in the valuation report only if the valuer believes that in the full circumstances it is appropriate.

## 10.6 Tolerance

The "without prejudice" agreement has been discussed. The SVD will have a range of values within which it will agree a valuation and outside of which it would agree a valuation if it was within a limited tolerance range, and then possibly only on a without prejudice basis. This tolerance range, in the order of £500–£750, would only be used in "clean" valuations that do not involve associated shareholdings where the tolerance limit could effectively be multiplied up.

## 10.7 Appeals

An appeal from a valuation determination by SVD is to the Special Commissioners and is brought in the same way as other tax appeals. The decision of the Commissioners on a matter of fact is final and conclusive but on a point of law their decision can be appealed against to the High Court.

# Appendix 1

# Model valuation report

Dear Mr Smith

*International Shipping Company Limited*
*Share Valuation at 1 July 1986*

We have been asked to prepare a valuation of 2,000 ordinary shares of £1 each in the company, which were transferred on 1 July 1986 by yourself (the transferor) to your son John Smith (the transferee).

*Purposes of the valuation*

The shares were transferred for no consideration and therefore are to be valued both for the purposes of capital transfer tax (CTT) and capital gains tax (CGT).

*Capital structure*

Before the transfer the fully paid issued share capital of 30,000 £1 shares was owned as to 29,000 by the transferor and 1,000 by Mrs M Smith (the transferor's wife).

*Basis of valuation*

The company is to be valued as a going concern. The company does not pay dividends and there is no intention to do so in the future. For CTT purposes it is the reduction in the value of the transferor's estate that has to be ascertained. The "earnings basis" of valuation is to be applied because the holdings by the transferor before and after the transfer are substantial majority holdings, in both cases exceeding 75%.

For CGT purposes, the value of the 2,000 shares is to be calculated on a dividend basis without regard being had to earnings because of the insignificance of the percentage of

190

shares transferred (6.66%), but with some regard being given to any surplus assets in the company, discounted heavily to reflect the shallow likelihood of receiving any actual benefit therefrom.

*Tax bases of valuation*

The shares, which are not quoted on a recognised stock exchange, are to be valued for *Capital Transfer Tax* in accordance with Capital Transfer Tax Act 1984 Part VI. Section 160 provides:

> "Except as otherwise provided by this part of this Act, the value at any time of any property shall for the purposes of this Act be the price which the property might reasonably be expected to fetch if sold in the open market at that time; but that price shall not be assumed to be reduced on the ground that the whole property is to be placed on the market at one and the same time."

and s.168 provides:

> "In determining the price which unquoted shares or securities might reasonably be expected to fetch if sold in the open market it shall be assumed that in that market there is available to any prospective purchaser of the shares or securities all the information which a prudent prospective purchaser might reasonably require if he were proposing to purchase them from a willing vendor by private treaty and at arm's length."

> "In this section "unquoted shares or securities" means shares or securities which are not quoted on a recognised stock exchange."

A reduction of 50% is available under Capital Transfer Tax Act 1984 s.104(1)(a) as the shares were part of a controlling interest in the company.

Under Capital Transfer Tax Act 1970 s.3(1) the chargeable transfer for capital transfer tax is the amount by which the transferor's estate is reduced by the transfer.

The transferor's wife holds 1,000 shares which are to be included for valuation purposes as related property under Capital Transfer Tax Act 1970 s.161.

The shares to be valued for CTT purposes are therefore:

| Before transfer | — transferor | 29,000 |
| | wife | 1,000 |
| | | 30,000 |
| After transfer | — transferor | 27,000 |
| | wife | 1,000 |
| | | 28,000 |

For *Capital Gains Tax* purposes the valuation provisions are contained in Capital Gains Tax Act 1979 s.150(1) and (2) which provides:

> "In this Act "market value" in relation to any assets means the price which those assets might reasonably be expected to fetch on a sale in the open market.

> In estimating the market value of any assets no reduction shall be made in the estimate on account of the estimate being made on the assumption that the whole of the assets is to be placed on the market at one and the same time."

And Capital Gains Tax Act 1979 s.152(3) which provides:

> "For the purposes of a determination it shall be assumed that, in the open market which is postulated for the purposes of that determination, there is available to any prospective purchaser of the asset in question all the information which a prudent prospective purchaser of the asset might reasonably require if he were proposing to purchase it from a willing vendor by private treaty and at arm's length."

For both CTT and CGT, various principles emerge from case law which assist in the interpretation of the statutory provisions:

(1) The test is what the purchaser would pay not what the then vendor would receive after costs.

(2) The market must be an open market without specially excluding anyone or specially including anyone: *IRC* v *Crossman.*

(3) Where the Articles of Association, as here, restrict the right to transfer, nevertheless the market must be open in the sense that it is assumed that the hypothetical purchaser will be entered on the register of members, but thereafter will hold the

shares subject to the restrictions in the articles: *IRC* v *Crossman.*

(4) The sales to be assumed are hypothetical sales and the fact that the transfer is by or to a director has to be disregarded: *Re Aschrott; Winter, Sutherlands Trustees* v *IRC; Duke of Buccleuch* v *IRC.*

(5) Directors owe no duty to a shareholder-vendor to disclose either orally or by way of documents the secrets of the boardroom: *Percival* v *Wright.*

(6) The directors would be under a positive duty not to disclose confidential information. What the directors would be prepared to disclose in a sale by private treaty is a question of fact: *Re Lynall, Lynall* v *IRC.*

(7) The hypothetical sale is deemed to take place at the time of the transfer: *Duke of Buccleuch* v *IRC.*

(8) Any subsequent placing of the ordinary shares, unless it were known to be in contemplation at the time of this transfer has no relevance since it would be a totally different sale in totally different conditions: *Earl of Ellesmere* v *IRC; IRC* v *Marr's Trustees.*

(9) Subsequent accounts can only be used to see what sort of forecast would have been given if the purchaser had asked for one, not to find out what actually happened: *Trustees of Johan Thomas Salvesen* v *IRC.*

## Articles of Association

The articles carry severe restrictions on the right to transfer shares, the directors have power to decline to register transfers and there is a pre-emption clause under which an independent "fair selling value" may be determined.

## Previous transfers

There has been no previous transfer of shares.

## Valuation assessment of shareholding

The shareholding to be valued represents a proportion of a controlling interest in a private unquoted company in the ship-broking, chartering and forwarding agents sector. The company is trading satisfactorily and there are no plans to liquidate the company in the foreseeable future. It is expected by the current owners and management that the company will continue to prosper.

*General economic conditions*

*Data:* (reported in FT of 2 July 1986):
At 1 July 1986 the FT-Actuaries Share Index for Shipping and Transport stood at 1517.09, 12 months previously this was 1075.28.

The FT-All Share Index was 820.28, 12 months previously this was 604.24.

Clearing banks base rate was 10%.

The yield on undated gilts was 8.91, 12 months previously this was 10.03.

The rate of exchange against the dollar in London was £1:$1.53.

*Outlook for the sector:* For some years the shipping and international transport industry has been in a depressed state. An improvement in this situation will first require a recovery in world markets which it is difficult to see in the immediate future. Although the company itself is buoyant by virtue of excellent management, it is clearly dependent upon factors largely outside its control in terms of demand, and therefore very high returns would be required to justify investment in this sector of the economy.

*Company financial history*

The company was incorporated on 1 September 1972 with an authorised and issued share capital of £30,000 fully paid. The company has traded satisfactorily since incorporation.

*Valuation approach*

The trading activities and performance of the company prior to 1980 were unexceptionable with commission never exceeding £130,000 and trading losses being made in each year. It is believed that a realistic view of the company's future cannot be taken by reference to those years.

Recent years' trading activities have been turbulent and considerable caution would be exercised by a prospective purchaser in taking the latest year's results as typical and an indicator of future years' profits.

Because of the peculiarity of a large windfall profit in 1985 and a loss in 1984, an average of averages has been used to identify what can be regarded as reasonable future maintainable profits.

*Earnings*

| Year ended 31 December | 1980 | 1981 | 1982 | 1983 | 1984 | 1985 |
|---|---|---|---|---|---|---|
| Commission received | 150,000 | 250,000 | 250,000 | 380,000 | 270,000 | 600,000 |
| Other income: | | | | | | |
| Rent | 1,000 | 1,000 | 1,000 | 1,000 | 2,000 | 2,000 |
| Foreign exchange | 1,000 | 1,000 | (3,000) | (15,000) | – | 1,000 |
| Sale of investments | 3,000 | – | – | 10,000 | 2,000 | – |
| Investment income & interest | 1,000 | 1,000 | 2,000 | 4,000 | 10,000 | 12,000 |
| Total per Profit & Loss Account | 156,000 | 253,000 | 250,000 | 380,000 | 284,000 | 615,000 |
| Net Profit/(Loss) | 4,000 | 25,000 | 40,000 | 35,000 | (20,000) | 200,000 |

*Adjustments*

| | 1980 | 1981 | 1982 | 1983 | 1984 | 1985 |
|---|---|---|---|---|---|---|
| Pension fund increase in 1985 over 1984 (200,000 - 30,000) at 75% (say) | | | | | | 127,000 |
| Sale of investments | (3,000) | – | – | (10,000) | (2,000) | – |
| Net trading profits | 1,000 | 25,000 | 40,000 | 25,000 | (22,000) | 327,000 |
| RPI at December | 275.6 | 308.8 | 325.5 | 342.8 | 358.5 | 378.9 |
| NTP adjusted to July 1986 RPI (384.7) | 1,395 | 31,145 | 47,275 | 28,056 | (23,608) | 332,006 |

*Notes:*

1. The pension fund extraordinary contribution in 1985 represented pre-tax appropriations of profits and for valuation purposes are not normal annual expenses. However, only 75% has been added back to the profits because ordinary annual contributions are a normal annual expense and these could reasonably vary considerably on a year by year basis.

2. Exchange profits and losses are the result of accounting requirements only. The trading activities are conducted in $US and it is not considered that there are risk factors attendant on the international trading. The results of the translation have not been removed from trading results for valuation purposes because it is considered that the likely purchaser of the shares in the company would be a UK resident and therefore conversion to sterling would possibly be a relevant factor in determining the benefit from dividends and earnings in the hands of the shareholders.

*Balance sheet and investments*

An analysis (see Appendix) of the company's investments that could be regarded as standing to one side of the business assets shows a decline in those assets as a percentage of the annual net asset value of the company. Nevertheless it is considered that the value at 31 December 1985 of the investments at 5.6% of the total net asset value of the company is material enough to be considered for bringing into the share valuation as an additional item. Cost of sales and liquidation is estimated at

£500, and because a minority shareholding is being valued the discount for uncertainty of realising the benefit in this case must be 75%. The value to be brought into account would therefore be:

Value of investments (ex leasehold property) — see Appendix, col (9): £15,000

    (£15,000 − £500) x 25% = £3,625.

In view of the high earnings value of the company, this amount is *de minimis* for an earnings basis of valuation, and in any event the income arising from these investments is included in the capitalised earnings.

The leasehold is regarded as a business asset that is not to be separated from the valuation of the company on a going concern basis because of the importance to the business of having premises of the same character and in the same locality.

### Interest arising and cash

Interest accruing to the company up to 1985 should be regarded as a concomitant of the business activities. The interest arises from cash on deposit and this cash is necessary to meet urgent demands for funds by ships and agents around the world. For 1985 the net current assets are considerably in excess of cash and bank balance.

### Profit trend — future maintainable earnings

A weighted average of the adjusted profits, first for the five years ended December 1984, and second for the five years ended December 1983 produce the following result:

| 1985 | 332,006 | x 5 | 1,660,030 | | |
| 1984 | (23,608) | x 4 | (94,432) | | |
| 1983 | 28,056 | x 3 | 84,168 | | |
| 1982 | 47,275 | x 2 | 94,550 | | |
| 1981 | 31,145 | x 1 | 31,145 | | |
| | | 15 | £1,775,461 | = | £118,364 |

| 1984 | (23,608) | x 5 | (118,040) | | |
| 1983 | 28,056 | x 4 | 112,224 | | |
| 1982 | 47,275 | x 3 | 141,825 | | |
| 1981 | 31,145 | x 2 | 62,290 | | |
| 1980 | 1,396 | x 1 | 1,396 | | |
| | | 15 | £199,695 | = | £13,313 |

The average which includes the 1985 results, over-emphasised the large exceptional profits for that year, but at the same time the average which takes into account the 1980 accounts and emphasises the year of loss is possibly understated in terms of what should be maintainable future profits. The average of the averages is:

$$118,364 + 13,313 = \frac{131,677}{2} = £65,838, \text{ say } £66,000.$$

Taking the last two years together, the average earnings would be:

$$332,006 + (23,608) = \frac{308,398}{2} = £154,199, \text{ say } £155,000$$

Maintainable future profits might then be estimated somewhere between these figures at, say, one quarter of the difference up on the lower figure, ie:

$$155,000 - 66,000 = 89,000/4 = £22,250$$
$$66,000 + 22,250 = 88,250, \text{ say } \underline{£90,000}.$$

Management projections for 1986 suggest profits of £190,000. It would be reasonable to increase the estimate of future maintainable profits by one-half of the difference up on £90,000, ie:

$$190,000 - 90,000 = \frac{100,000}{2} = £50,000$$
$$90,000 + 50,000 = \underline{£140,000}.$$

*Comparison with quoted companies*

The Price to Earnings ratio on 1 July 1986 for quoted companies in the shipping and transport sectors are too at variance with each other to draw a conclusion for the purpose of this valuation.

*Capital Transfer Tax valuation — earnings basis*

The view has already been expressed that a high return would be expected, especially when there is no substantial asset-backing equivalent to that of the quoted shipping companies.

A Price to Earnings ratio of 5:5 would appear to be realistic in terms of the wider economic risk, but in view of the management efficiency which should not alter on this share transfer, this might be advanced to 6.

Corporation tax rates for the future may be taken to be 35%.

|  | £ |
|---|---|
| Pre-tax future maintainable profits | 140,000 |
| Less: corporation tax @ 35% | 49,000 |
| Anticipated maintainable profits post tax | £91,000 |
| PER @ 6 | 546,000 |
| Less: discount for non-marketability @ 25% | 136,500 |
|  | £409,500 |
| Value per share on earnings basis (30,000 shares) | £13.65 |
| For Capital Transfer Tax shares transferred 2,000 @ £13.65 | £27,300 |
| Less Business relief at 50% | 13,650 |
| Chargeable transfer | £13,650 |

## *Capital Gains Tax valuation — Dividend basis*

For Capital Gains Tax the dividends basis would apply

|  | £ |
|---|---|
| Anticipated maintainable profits post-tax | 91,000 |
| Reasonable distribution, say 1/3rd | 30,333 |
| Grossed for ACT @ 3/7 | 43,333 |
| Required yield — probably 12% Capitalised value | 316,111 |
| Discount for non-payment of dividends — 50% | 180,555 |
| Capitalised dividends | 180,555 |
| Additional asset-backing £3,625 (already discounted) | 3,625 |
|  | 184,180 |
| Discount for non-marketability @ 40% | 72,222 |
|  | 111,958 |
| Value of 2,000 of 30,000 shares | £7,464 |

# Appendix: Investments

| | (1) | (2) | (3) | (4) | (5) | (6) | (7) | (8) | (9) | (10) |
|---|---|---|---|---|---|---|---|---|---|---|
| | | Leasehold property* | | | Investments† | | | Balance Sheet Net asset value after revaluation surpluses (Cols 1, 4 & 7)‡ | Value of Investments (ex. leasehold property) (Col. 6) | Value of Investments (Col. 9) as %age of revalued balance sheet (Col. 8) |
| | Balance sheet Net asset value | Book Value | Estimated Realisable Market Value | Reval-uation Surplus | Balance Sheet Book Value | Esti-mated Realisable Market Value | Reval-uation Surplus | | | |
| 1985 | 200,000 | 40,000 | 100,000 | 60,000 | 8,000 | 15,000 | 7,000 | 267,000 | 15,000 | 5.6% |
| 1984 | 80,000 | 40,000 | 80,000 | 40,000 | 4,000 | 10,000 | 6,000 | 126,000 | 10,000 | 7.9% |
| 1983 | 100,000 | 40,000 | 70,000 | 30,000 | 4,000 | 9,000 | 5,000 | 135,000 | 9,000 | 6.7% |
| 1982 | 80,000 | 40,000 | 60,000 | 20,000 | 12,000 | 20,000 | 8,000 | 108,000 | 20,000 | 18.5% |
| 1981 | 80,000 | 40,000 | 50,000 | 10,000 | 8,000 | 8,000 | – | 90,000 | 8,000 | 8.8% |
| 1980 | 20,000 | 40,000 | 40,000 | – | 7,000 | (4,000) | 3,000 | 17,000 | 4,000 | 23.5% |

*The leasehold property (Cols 2 - 4) has been valued by Jones & Co (Auctioneers, Valuers and Estate Agents) at April 1986 at £100,000. Its annual market value each year back to 1980 (when purchased) has been estimated from that valuation.

†The estimated realisable market values of the investments (Col. 6) have been provided by a director and are recorded in the notes to the annual accounts.

‡The revalued balance sheet (Col. 8) does not include any revaluation of plant, machinery, fixtures and fittings which are estimated to have the same value as their book value for a going-concern, it therefore represents the full net asset value of the business as a going concern excluding goodwill.

# Appendix 2

**These Indices are the joint compilation of the Financial Times,
the Institute of Actuaries and the Faculty of Actuaries**

| EQUITY GROUPS & SUB-SECTIONS | | | | | | | Weds Oct 29 | Tues Oct 28 | Mon Oct 27 | Year ago (approx.) |
|---|---|---|---|---|---|---|---|---|---|---|
| Figures in parentheses show number of stocks per section | Index No. | Day's Change % | Est. Earnings Yield% (Max.) | Gross Div. Yield% (ACT at 29%) | Est. P/E Ratio (Net) | xd adj. 1986 to date | Index No. | Index No. | Index No. | Index No. |
| 1 CAPITAL GOODS (211) | 658.17 | +0.9 | 9.21 | 3.88 | 13.81 | 15.51 | 652.59 | 645.09 | 643.50 | 556.05 |
| 2 Building Materials (27) | 797.36 | +1.4 | 9.10 | 3.67 | 13.87 | 17.46 | 786.28 | 776.63 | 775.46 | 625.01 |
| 3 Contracting, Construction (30) | 1106.48 | +0.1 | 7.40 | 4.19 | 19.05 | 28.80 | 1105.48 | 1085.88 | 1080.16 | 952.52 |
| 4 Electricals (12) | 1757.73 | +0.8 | 8.25 | 4.76 | 15.70 | 53.27 | 1744.44 | 1734.28 | 1723.64 | 1554.28 |
| 5 Electronics (38) | 1417.46 | +0.1 | 9.99 | 2.87 | 13.33 | 29.35 | 1415.93 | 1400.74 | 1393.06 | 1285.35 |
| 6 Mechanical Engineering (60) | 365.29 | +1.6 | 10.80 | 4.51 | 11.81 | 9.79 | 359.40 | 355.28 | 355.72 | 322.56 |
| 7 Metals and Metal Forming (7) | 333.14 | — | 9.58 | 4.23 | 13.13 | 7.39 | 333.09 | 328.68 | 328.10 | 229.45 |
| 8 Motors (16) | 255.14 | +0.3 | 10.33 | 4.01 | 11.25 | 5.67 | 254.31 | 252.42 | 253.63 | 194.56 |
| 10 Other Industrial Materials (21) | 1214.35 | +1.3 | 7.34 | 4.44 | 16.11 | 29.58 | 1198.67 | 1185.36 | 1180.79 | 1022.23 |
| 20 CONSUMER GROUP (185) | 929.22 | +0.7 | 8.06 | 3.34 | 15.64 | 16.70 | 922.52 | 912.70 | 913.04 | 756.74 |
| 22 Brewers and Distillers (22) | 951.46 | +1.8 | 9.23 | 3.38 | 13.33 | 14.91 | 934.41 | 926.85 | 919.28 | 781.99 |
| 25 Food Manufacturing (24) | 708.07 | +0.2 | 9.46 | 3.85 | 13.76 | 14.49 | 706.96 | 701.53 | 699.33 | 549.00 |
| 26 Food Retailing (16) | 1866.42 | −0.4 | 6.25 | 2.80 | 22.26 | 36.21 | 1874.09 | 1865.26 | 1882.06 | 1723.53 |
| 27 Health and Household Products (10) | 1522.83 | +1.3 | 6.38 | 2.49 | 18.99 | 12.84 | 1503.32 | 1480.11 | 1477.08 | 1169.28 |
| 29 Leisure (27) | 922.17 | +0.7 | 8.04 | 4.42 | 16.50 | 25.08 | 916.18 | 911.67 | 914.83 | 737.77 |
| 32 Publishing & Printing (15) | 2594.57 | +0.5 | 7.16 | 4.36 | 18.10 | 55.86 | 2581.59 | 2450.74 | 2434.74 | 1895.99 |
| 33 Packaging and Paper (14) | 475.09 | +2.9 | 7.11 | 3.47 | 18.29 | 10.54 | 461.61 | 452.76 | 455.86 | 369.65 |
| 34 Stores (38) | 854.36 | +0.4 | 6.97 | 3.06 | 19.45 | 13.98 | 851.19 | 849.91 | 856.19 | 789.87 |
| 35 Textiles (17) | 526.40 | +0.5 | 9.72 | 3.75 | 11.90 | 10.11 | 524.01 | 517.20 | 518.55 | 365.76 |
| 36 Tobaccos (2) | 1268.88 | +0.6 | 13.02 | 4.08 | 8.44 | 36.99 | 1261.86 | 1235.14 | 1226.89 | 835.77 |
| 41 OTHER GROUPS (87) | 781.31 | +0.7 | 8.61 | 4.09 | 14.97 | 17.35 | 776.25 | 769.02 | 767.06 | 711.97 |
| 42 Chemicals (20) | 1001.65 | +1.6 | 8.77 | 4.32 | 13.86 | 29.89 | 986.29 | 979.07 | 974.87 | 691.51 |
| 44 Office Equipment (4) | 241.05 | — | 7.71 | 4.41 | 15.68 | 7.55 | 241.03 | 241.36 | 241.36 | 229.58 |
| 45 Shipping and Transport (13) | 1536.20 | +2.3 | 7.88 | 4.30 | 16.18 | 41.58 | 1501.83 | 1490.50 | 1494.24 | 1362.44 |
| 47 Telephone Networks (2) | 762.73 | −0.1 | 11.24 | 4.82 | 12.15 | 16.67 | 763.79 | 754.60 | 755.40 | 891.47 |
| 48 Miscellaneous (48) | 1091.53 | +0.4 | 6.18 | 3.12 | 20.32 | 16.84 | 1087.13 | 1076.80 | 1069.98 | 898.96 |
| 49 INDUSTRIAL GROUP(483) | 828.57 | +0.7 | 8.47 | 3.65 | 14.99 | 16.85 | 822.49 | 813.82 | 812.99 | 699.71 |
| 51 Oil & Gas (17) | 1350.56 | +3.1 | 12.10 | 6.43 | 10.18 | 62.40 | 1309.35 | 1318.11 | 1340.58 | 1150.45 |
| 59 500 SHARE INDEX(500) | 872.97 | +1.0 | 8.89 | 4.00 | 14.21 | 20.44 | 864.21 | 856.80 | 857.72 | 738.17 |
| 61 FINANCIAL GROUP (118) | 607.72 | +0.9 | — | 4.66 | — | 16.78 | 602.07 | 600.88 | 600.12 | 523.93 |
| 62 Banks (8) | 663.52 | +1.9 | 18.98 | 5.52 | 7.23 | 23.94 | 651.23 | 649.35 | 646.66 | 528.47 |
| 65 Insurance (Life) (9) | 814.82 | +1.0 | — | 4.78 | — | 27.29 | 806.88 | 806.93 | 805.74 | 787.69 |
| 66 Insurance (Composite) (7) | 475.18 | −0.4 | — | 4.57 | — | 10.93 | 476.92 | 478.09 | 480.75 | 399.27 |
| 67 Insurance (Brokers) (9) | 1308.49 | +2.2 | 7.51 | 3.96 | 17.40 | 35.33 | 1279.80 | 1269.39 | 1262.81 | 1209.40 |
| 68 Merchant Banks (12) | 344.16 | +0.7 | — | 4.16 | — | 5.98 | 341.78 | 342.50 | 341.72 | 287.70 |
| 69 Property (49) | 789.86 | +0.2 | 5.72 | 3.57 | 22.91 | 14.35 | 787.99 | 781.99 | 782.38 | 696.31 |
| 70 Other Financial (24) | 355.27 | +0.3 | 9.06 | 4.44 | 13.42 | 9.06 | 354.19 | 353.27 | 354.11 | 310.30 |
| 71 Investment Trusts (99) | 820.23 | +1.1 | — | 2.77 | — | 13.75 | 811.67 | 807.44 | 803.68 | 634.47 |
| 81 Mining Finance (2) | 324.05 | +1.0 | 9.69 | 4.95 | 12.13 | 11.30 | 320.77 | 322.68 | 324.79 | 251.96 |
| 91 Overseas Traders (13) | 754.54 | — | 10.23 | 5.84 | 11.67 | 27.22 | 754.56 | 745.43 | 732.35 | 590.04 |
| 99 ALL-SHARE INDEX (732) | 800.61 | +1.0 | — | 4.08 | — | 19.21 | 792.72 | 786.97 | 787.28 | 675.20 |

| | Index No. | Day's Change | Day's High | Day's Low | Oct 29 | Oct 28 | Oct 27 | Oct 24 | Oct 23 | Year ago |
|---|---|---|---|---|---|---|---|---|---|---|
| FT-SE 100 SHARE INDEX ♦ | 1615.8 | +18.8 | 1617.2 | 1596.9 | 1597.0 | 1583.6 | 1586.2 | 1577.1 | 1572.5 | 1384.8 |

## FIXED INTEREST

| PRICE INDICES | Thurs Oct 30 | Day's change % | Weds Oct 29 | xd adj. today | xd adj. 1986 to date |
|---|---|---|---|---|---|
| **British Government** | | • | | | |
| 1 5 years | 118.86 | +0.03 | 118.82 | — | 9.57 |
| 2 5-15 years | 129.17 | +0.07 | 129.08 | — | 11.61 |
| 3 Over 15 years | 134.82 | +0.10 | 134.69 | — | 11.43 |
| 4 Irredeemables | 146.23 | +0.43 | 145.60 | — | 13.34 |
| 5 All stocks | 127.77 | +0.07 | 127.68 | — | 11.01 |
| **Index-Linked** | | | | | |
| 6 5 years | 113.13 | −0.03 | 113.16 | — | 2.00 |
| 7 Over 5 years | 110.23 | −0.11 | 110.35 | — | 2.84 |
| 8 All stocks | 110.66 | −0.10 | 110.77 | — | 2.69 |
| 9 Debentures & Loans | 111.20 | +0.24 | 110.97 | 0.05 | 9.85 |
| 10 Preference | 79.14 | −0.42 | 79.48 | — | 5.41 |

| AVERAGE GROSS REDEMPTION YIELDS | | | Thurs Oct 30 | Weds Oct 29 | Year ago (approx.) |
|---|---|---|---|---|---|
| **British Government** | | | | | |
| 1 Low | 5 years | | 9.81 | 9.79 | 9.95 |
| 2 Coupons | 15 years | | 10.41 | 10.43 | 10.29 |
| 3 | 25 years | | 10.42 | 10.44 | 10.22 |
| 4 Medium | 5 years | | 11.25 | 11.26 | 10.81 |
| 5 Coupons | 15 years | | 10.77 | 10.78 | 10.55 |
| 6 | 25 years | | 10.40 | 10.42 | 10.22 |
| 7 High | 5 years | | 11.31 | 11.32 | 10.92 |
| 8 Coupons | 15 years | | 10.96 | 10.96 | 10.70 |
| 9 | 25 years | | 10.58 | 10.60 | 10.38 |
| 10 Irredeemables | | | 10.18 | 10.23 | 9.77 |
| **Index-Linked** | | | | | |
| 11 Inflat'n rate 5% | | 5 yrs | 4.36 | 4.33 | 0.0 |
| 12 Inflat'n rate 5% | | Over 5 yrs | 3.83 | 3.82 | 0.0 |
| 13 Inflat'n rate 10% | | 5 yrs | 2.95 | 2.91 | 0.0 |
| 14 Inflat'n rate 10% | | Over 5 yrs | 3.66 | 3.65 | 0.0 |
| 15 Debs & | 5 years | | 11.59 | 11.45 | 11.20 |
| 16 Loans | 15 years | | 11.55 | 11.60 | 11.20 |
| 17 | 25 years | | 11.51 | 11.55 | 11.20 |
| 18 Preference | | | 11.63 | 11.58 | 11.84 |

♦Opening index 1596.9; 10 am 1601.1; 11 am 1599.6; Noon 1599.9; 1 pm 1600.2; 2 pm 1604.9; 3 pm 1614.7; 3.30 pm 1616.9; 4 pm 1614.2

† Flat yield. Highs and lows record, base dates, values and constituent changes are published in Saturday issues. A new list of constituents is available from the Publishers, the Financial Times, Bracken House, Cannon Street, London EC4P 4BY, price 15p, by post 28p.

Reproduced with the permission of the Financial Times

# Index